D1010952

The Real Nureyev

Rudolf Nureyev
17 March 1938 – 6 January 1993

CAROLYN SOUTAR

THE REAL NUREYEV

Thomas Dunne Books
St. Martin's Press
New York

THOMAS DUNNE BOOKS.
An imprint of St. Martin's Press.

www.stmartins.com

Library of Congress Cataloging-in-Publication Data

Soutar, Carolyn.
The real Nureyev : an intimate memoir of ballet's greatest hero / Carolyn Soutar
p. cm.
Originally published: Edinburgh : Mainstream, 2004.
Includes bibliographical references (p. 187) and index (p. 189).
ISBN 0-312-34097-4
EAN 978-0-312-34097-1
1. Nureyev, Rudolf, 1938– 2. Ballet dancers—Russia (Federation)—Biography. 3. Ballet dancers—Great Britain—Biography. I. Title.

GV1785.N8S68 2006
792.8'028'092—dc22
[B]

2005051954

First published in Great Britain by
Mainstream Publishing Company (Edinburgh) Ltd

First Edition: January 2006

10 9 8 7 6 5 4 3 2 1

Acknowledgements

Many people spent precious hours of their time helping me with this book. HRH Princess Michael of Kent, Lord Rix, Robert Tracy, Violette Verdy, Yoko Morishita, Bill Akers, Roger Myers, Harriet Walter, Ted Murphy, Adam Harrison and Pamela Foulkes were wonderful to talk to and were generous in sharing their memories.

I have used generic names for the crew at the London Coliseum. There were over 40 of them, working in shifts and bringing huge personalities, talent and a love of the theatre to my time there from 1972–85. So I decided not to list all the 'Pauls', 'Steves', 'Martins', 'Charlies', 'Brians', 'Teds' and 'Alans', nor have I mentioned the wonderful sets of fathers and sons working together, but they are all in here in spirit.

Early in the 1900s, Sir Oswald Stoll named the London Coliseum as a *Coliseum* not a Roman Colosseum and, whilst confusing, the spelling is correct.

When I was working with English National Opera, the auditorium changed from a sea of red seats to green or turquoise ones, and now with its renovation they have returned to red. The house curtain has now changed to imperial purple.

My thanks to Noriko Davidson for her enthusiasm and immaculate translations, Andrew Killian for his support and research work and also to John Ezard.

I have adored working on this book and reliving the memories of working with Rudolf Nureyev. Parents and friends gave me confidence and encouragement. I am so grateful to Ailsa, my editor, for her patience and guidance. Without my agent, Peter Cox, this project would not exist, and his humour and clear vision have supported me throughout this wonderful experience.

Contents

PROLOGUE

Russian Roulette

10 JUNE 1980

There is a moment in the life of a theatre when the stillness prior to the arrival of the cast and crew becomes electric, when footsteps echo down the wings and doors bang way off in the distance.

If you glance at your watch, it is usually somewhere between six fifteen and seven in the evening. Now add the quiet swish of a foot extending to the right and back, backwards and forwards, slowly then rapidly, an accentuated thump of the ball of the foot hitting the floor, and you are listening to the sound of a ballet dancer warming up.

If I turn my head slightly to my right, even now I can see not just any ballet dancer but Rudolf Nureyev, holding on to a lighting ladder by the proscenium arch of the London Coliseum.

He is wearing a woolly hat set at a rakish angle, a blue knitted jumpsuit negligently slides from his shoulders over a white torn-sleeved T-shirt and on his feet are battered, much-abused white dance shoes with greying elastic across his instep.

He is two feet away from me, whilst I sit in the stage manager's prompt corner, or desk, waiting to call the 'half' – 35 minutes to the start of the show – over the Tannoy. He stops, looks at me and as I smile in recognition he says, 'Let's see if Old Galoshes can dance tonight,' then waits for my certain response.

'Old Galoshes? You are joking?' I gasp as his whole face creases into a wide smile. I am horrified at this expression, this idol comparing himself to a lumpy old Wellington boot.

'Why Old Galoshes?'

'It means someone good, but dancing badly,' he explains, and, still smiling at me, laughing at my shocked expression, he returns to his warm-up.

The cables and ropes in the flys creak eerily and I sit back and watch my own first private performance by this icon.

At the bottom of the lighting ladder sit a pair of clogs, a towel and a flask of tea. Rudolf's: still life on black lino.

Something catches my eye and I look up. Inevitably, a paper petal or snowflake floats languidly down from the grid high above the stage and lands centre stage right on the dancer's turning spot. Someone shouts upstage, seemingly miles away. I can't make out what they are saying. The large black relay speakers hum quietly but without the sound of the orchestra tuning or audience murmur. Black stage lights creak and rattle above Rudolf's head in time to his leg movements, whilst I sit mesmerised by the fluid movement of his right arm to the side, above his head and then, with feet close together crossed in fourth position and his body fully bowed forward in obeisance, he rests his curved hand on the black floor of the empty stage.

Rudolf changes the pace of his warm-up and moves smoothly into more energetic leg extensions and stretching, inhaling the backstage smells: over 100 years of dust, size (horse glue used to firm the canvas on scenic flats), hemp, fire-retardant spray and old scenery, and today the basement under-stage canteen provides aromatherapy for us on stage, the pungent smell of shepherd's pie, carrots and cabbage wafting up through the dip traps, where the many cables are plugged safely out of the way under the stage floor.

There is the sound of determined footsteps coming down the wings on the other side of the stage 50 feet away – the fireman. He shouts to no one in particular, 'Iron coming in', and then there is a loud clang that signals the huge functional brown iron fire curtain being lowered or, in the rather scary theatrical parlance, being 'dropped'. I reach for the large handle that operates the house curtain and pull it towards me to raise the curtain before the iron rests on it.

The iron curtain arrives and shudders to a halt, then there is another shout, 'Iron going out'. The test for the evening is over until the interval when the curtain will be brought in again to dull the sounds of the scene changes and to show the public by law that it works. Metallic thumps echo down from the flys, as a flyman loads up a weights cradle in the counterweight system in order that the scenery or cloths can be flown in safely by one person.

Rudolf waits for the sound of the fireman walking upstage and away. Then he turns, crossing to a point slightly upstage of centre. He's standing now, hands on hips, looking at his feet, thinking.

Centre stage and waiting.

He prepares, psyches himself up, chest out, head high, arms out to his side, then jumps and turns to land with a thump. Dissatisfied, he stops and hands go back on hips, waiting to try again.

So this is the dancer that audiences hero-worship and both men and women love from afar? The defector, the exotic Tartar famously born on the Trans-Siberian Express, who described his incredibly harsh childhood to me as 'selling pencils in the mud', as the family scraped together money to survive. He is now such a household name that anyone in the world could tell you at least one thing about him, even if it is only about his famous appearance on *The Muppet Show* in 'Swine Lake'. They all know his name, although to some it has become the Morecambe and Wise 'Randolf Near Enough' or Festival Ballet's rumoured 'Rudolf Never Off'.

This is a man who dances even now at the age of 42 over 250 performances a year, compared to the younger Nijinsky's 50. But the same man who answers '3' when asked by a reporter to assess, out of the 250, how many of those performances he's happy with.

I'm awestruck.

Rudolf Nureyev is standing centre stage looking into the vast cavern of the empty theatre, just as I have done over the years. Standing looking during endless lighting rehearsals, where the lighting states are painstakingly created and plotted for operas and ballets. In all my time here I have never seen the famous ghost of a First World War soldier who reputedly takes his seat in the upper circle to watch his sweetheart perform, as she did the night before he went to the Front, where he was killed.

As I watch Rudolf, I wonder if he and the ghost have ever silently 'saluted' one another, enigma to enigma, in these private moments.

I hear Rudolf take a deep breath and he stares straight out into the darkness ahead. In front of him there's an empty auditorium, a sea of blue seats, waiting to be filled with his fans. The lighting is harsh, cold and unflattering. No theatrical stage lights, just 'overhead workers' and 'fluorescent tubes'. I check mutely with Rudolf whether he minds if I drop the house curtain, communicating in sign language. I take the silent raised eyebrow and shrug as a go-ahead, so I push the large lever away from me, and the 'tabs', the huge 30-metre-wide house curtain, slowly comes in.

There are footsteps now in front of the tabs, a vast expanse of turquoise velvet. There's a shoulder-height line of body make-up visible on them from the weeks of front-of-curtain calls for dancers, as they slide out for their recognition and adulation. The front-of-house manager on the other side of the tabs now announces to the staff the name of the ballet being performed, *Don Quixote* – performed by the Zurich Ballet – the running times of each act, the duration of each interval and calls. Then there's a routine exchange of shouts.

'Are you clear in the balcony?'

Miles away, someone yells, 'Yes, thank you!'

'Are you clear in the upper circle?'

A chorus of 'Yes!'

'Are you clear in the circle?'

'Missing one!'

'Are you clear in the stalls?'

Loud calls of 'Yes!'

There is a nightly rehearsal for an emergency evacuation of the 2,232 members of the audience. I'm used to it but Nureyev looks impatient, irritated, unnaturally still.

'Thank you, ladies and gentlemen.'

The footsteps leave and we have silence again.

Rudolf Nureyev starts to practise his turns, some perfect, some quite rough, with ruthless self-discipline; but he watches as the master carpenter in charge of the crew and the scenery for the night leaves his office and the door bangs loudly halfway up the stage's right wings. The master carpenter comes down to see me in the prompt corner. 'Everything all right, Carolyn?' he asks.

This is everyday stuff. 'Fine, thanks, Ted.' I notice that Rudolf is watching and listening, glaring as he tries to focus on his moves.

'All right, Rudi?' shouts Ted with a wave and a laugh to the world's greatest ballet dancer, who is staring and flaring his nostrils at Ted as he walks back upstage and through the swing doors.

It is amazing how a pair of flared Tartar nostrils can hit you on the back of the head from 50 feet away on a bad day.

A piercing cormorant cry comes over the huge black relay speakers in the wings. We are no longer alone. An oboe is warming up in the orchestra pit. Then comes the elastic-band reverberating sound of the timpani drums being tuned, and conversations from the orchestra players are relayed on to the stage.

Rudolf Nureyev stops and stares at the ground, hands on hips, feet splayed, weight on one hip, sweat pouring off his face and chest on to the floor. He uses his fingers to wipe his nostrils and forehead, and shakes the moisture from his hand onto the stage. Then he looks up to see who I'm talking to. Always watching. It is just a member of the property staff who wants to know how long 'Rudi' will be and where he wants his rehearsal barre in the wings. Do I know? It is the first time I've been party to this ritual and I have no idea. Instead I suggest that he comes back in ten minutes to see what is going on then.

The floor reverberates as Rudolf starts his jumps. We are lucky this summer. London Festival Ballet (now called English National Ballet) have left their ballet floor, a huge false floor that sits over the many theatrical traps, the parallel lines of the Coliseum's double revolve and various other toe traps for dancers, but the sound of even the slightest ballerina landing is still a surprise to the uninitiated.

'Fuck me, Rudi. Can't you get higher than that?' A loud Australian accent permeates from a short man crossing the stage, one of the crew.

'*Pisstushka*.'

I hear Rudolf bark this reply. He always liked to use such language to shock and to see the reaction. I don't speak Russian but I can work out what it means.

'Silly Russian poof,' the Australian laughs back.

Oh God, don't tell me that I am going to have an 'incident' on my first day. I poke my head round the corner of a flat and see that both are grinning broadly at one another. Old sparring partners, I assume. After all, he's been dancing in London for nearly 20 years and has met many of the technicians before with several different ballet companies.

And then, just to show that he can do it, Rudolf prepares and does the jump again. It is perfect. I am watching open mouthed and we all catch our breath. Surely at 42 Old Galoshes couldn't repeat that? But this time, apparently miraculously, the magic appears again and Rudolf Nureyev, the superb dancer, not Old Galoshes, spins, astonishing everyone.

'Come on, my son, we can all do that,' shouts another stagehand, while clumsily, and rather less than convincingly, trying to reprise Rudolf's turns. He's an old hand at taunting Nureyev, an ex-dancer who can just about manage one revolution before toppling over.

Rudolf is laughing. He obviously loves the camaraderie. He smiles and continues cooling down, focused and in his element with an audience, especially this down-to-earth assembly of workers attempting to wind him up with good humour. This is the ribald part of the routine, which everyone seems to enjoy before the beauty of the dance and the music. He is in his element sparring with the workers who accept him as just another bloke, nothing special, and he appears to revel in this acceptance.

'Heads up!' A warning cry from the high fly floor.

'You're all right, Dave, bring 'em in.'

'Rudi, stay where you are, mate, cloths coming in,' and Brian, one of the crew, moves on to the stage to stand protectively by Rudolf as the drapes and cloths that transform our bare, black-boxed world into a Spanish village are slowly flown in. We all turn and watch as the 'legs', the narrower cloths, slink their way over the tall, black masking flats, then laugh resignedly as inevitably one of the borders hooks itself over another in the middle of the stage. It is right in the audience's line of sight and it needs to be rescued.

'Hold up, Dave. The number three border's fouled.'

The grid is cluttered with lighting bars, then black masking borders to hide the lighting bars and on top of these are the scenic borders to hide the black borders. It only takes the slightest of updraughts to wreak havoc and give us an unsightly mess.

An enormous bamboo pole is wobbled on to the stage by one of the crew and we all become the living embodiment of the old joke, 'How many people does it take to watch a man with a stick?' Answer, quite a few, including the world's most famous ballet dancer.

The errant border is flicked back into place.

There is an odd rumbling noise as one of the props staff rolls a huge magnet over the stage. This is a final check for any nails or tacks that may be lurking on the stage and could harm a dancer.

It is one interruption too many.

Rudolf Nureyev walks off the stage towards me, puts his feet into his clogs, mops his dripping face, chest and neck, drapes his towel around his neck, picks up his flask of tea and takes a last look at the stage before shuffle-walking indolently upstage towards his dressing-room. He smells of heat and sweat, and barely looks at me. I am mesmerised by this rear view of him as he disappears up the wings, with sinuous glistening shoulders, dripping wet hair, knitted hat, and rolled-down jumpsuit sitting over the widest part of his hips, and wonder how he will transform from this ragamuffin into a romantic prince in a few minutes' time.

As I watch Rudolf Nureyev disappear into his dressing-room, I say to myself that I am going to remember all of this, every single moment, just in case I never work with him again after this year.

I call the half-hour over the Tannoy and Rudolf's dresser arrives to snatch, rather imperiously, the huge Rolex watch, Rudolf's, which I am holding out to him. It has been left on the desk where I sit. Now I have 15 minutes to myself and leave to see whether the aroma of food from the canteen can possibly tempt me. I face the old conundrum of knowing that while I am not actually hungry right at this moment, I will be in three hours' time just as I leave to go home, and by then the canteen will be long shut.

A few weeks ago, I had the opportunity to laze on a lovely beach and enjoy daily doses of unappetising lukewarm moussaka, accompanied by glasses of Retsina and Demestica on my annual escape to the Greek islands – along with most of the English National Opera on their annual pilgrimage to the sun. We used to joke about meeting everyone from the company at Athens airport, all of us trying to escape from one another but ending up briefly in exactly the same place, before disappearing to our favourite island and sanctuary for the next few weeks.

But I know now that I made the right choice, to stay put, to be here in 1980 with the Nureyev Festival and Zurich Ballet.

The Nureyev Festivals had been running at the Coliseum for a few years. These seasons were a huge attraction for ballet fans. They ran for sometimes as many as six weeks, featured many international ballet companies, and starred, of course, Rudolf Nureyev. The crew had told me how exciting and glamorous these ballet seasons were, and how much they enjoyed meeting the different companies that came over to dance with the legendary Nureyev. They had also told me about his reputation for being impossible, unpredictable, that he hated women and that he threw furniture as well as tantrums. Whilst I had the feeling that there was a lot of 'winding-up' going on with the stories of his temper, I was still anxious. It was going to be an interesting time and it was a welcome change after nine months of opera and our usual routine. It was my turn to experience this phenomenon first hand: a once-in-a-lifetime opportunity.

Dancers begin to drift down onto the stage, leaving leg-warmers and shoes in small piles in the wings. Disembodied legs appear from behind 30-foot-high black masking flats, which wobble alarmingly as bends and stretches are practised again.

'Careful, gorgeous, mind you don't pull that over.' One of the crew hastens to the side of an extremely wobbly flat as a tiny ballerina hangs on to the brace at the back whilst practising her extensions.

Ballerinas put one elegant pointe after another into rosin trays that are scattered in the wings, the rosin used to prevent their shoes from slipping, and sit, legs akimbo on the floor, tying their ribbons like a frieze of Degas paintings.

It has been a long couple of days already. Yesterday, Sunday morning, huge wagons arrived at the stage door from exotic locations. Introductions were made between visiting chiefs of various departments and the load-in crew got to work, taking out huge hanging cloths, scenery, wicker baskets full of shoes, wigs and make-up boxes, and rail after rail of costumes. And then, this morning, there had been a class on stage to familiarise the company with the layout of the Coliseum. But no Nureyev. Just barres, bodies and feet, and sweating dancers wrapped up protecting their cold muscles inside whilst it is a glorious June day outside.

I asked the visiting stage manager if Nureyev had a late call and he just said, 'That's Rudi', implying that there were different rules for this dancer, ones of his own making.

The barres were cleared from the stage after an hour or so and the stage set for a full orchestral rehearsal of the ballet. This was my first introduction to *Don Quixote*: windmills, pantomime horses, comedy and a feast of colour, fun and toe-tapping music. The *Don Quixote* that was Nureyev's 'baby', his production with his choreography. But there was still no sign of the man himself. Then, as I watched the final piece being placed, I could feel the atmosphere change behind me.

Rudolf Nureyev had arrived in street clothes. Knee boots, tan suede trousers, a multicoloured knitted jacket and leather cap. He walked straight across the stage, greeting people perfunctorily, glanced towards me and went to his dressing-room. The visiting stage manager and I exchanged shrugs and the rehearsal continued.

After a few minutes had passed and I thought that he had had time to settle himself in his dressing-room, I decided to go and introduce myself and check that he had everything he needed. I suddenly realised that I was actually nervous. I had done this hundreds of times but I was almost shaking.

The door to the number-one dressing-room was open and he was organising his make-up, towels, hairsprays, brushes and costumes. There were umpteen pairs of ballet shoes laid out in a row on the dressing table itself. He was courteous, smiled, asked me to put a rehearsal barre in the wings for him and to check that there was one every day in the stage-right wings, morning, afternoon and evening. As I left, he asked me to repeat my name, 'Carolyn'.

'Caroline,' he echoed, distractedly mispronouncing in that soft extraordinary voice with that accent that everyone remembers, just for a second making a flicker of eye contact. I was never going to correct him after that pronunciation had undulated over me.

'Caroline,' he said again, more confidently this time, and smiling. I smiled back. This was going to be all right. So where was this tyrant and ogre that I'd heard so much about? In his place was a quiet professional, slightly distant, perhaps even a little shy.

He was so unlike what I'd been led to expect. From the rumours I'd heard from the crew and friends who had worked with him, I had expected an unapproachable, uncontrollable, egotistical tyrant. I had not anticipated charm.

Within minutes, he'd returned to the stage to walk through with Yoko Morishita, the prima ballerina, the pas de deux from *Don Quixote*. There was a sharp dismissal of Yoko's leg-warmers, which I found amusing as he was still in his street clothes, including the leather cap. She removed them.

I learned over the years to spot the difference with his partners. The ones that he handled like spun glass, who were light as air and the perfect weight and size for him at his age, and the ones that were too heavy, too tall, that he appeared to stand back from and almost say, 'You're on your own!' as they landed with a thump, unaided by him. This one he handled delicately and with the utmost care, Yoko listening avidly to everything Rudolf said to her.

They walked through the mountain-top scene in front of the windmill and the erotic movement on the red silk scarf of two lovers lying together and sinuously wrapping the red silk around them.

They stopped for a moment to talk to the conductor. As everything was running well, I took my chance to leave the stage and collect some coffees for myself and the visiting stage management.

On my way back, I was stunned to find the crew leaving with their coats on. When I questioned them, they told me that one of the company had said that they 'weren't needed any more'.

I had a horrible feeling about this, a really awful feeling. Sure enough, I was greeted by a group of worried faces as they wanted to change to the next scene but there was no crew. 'Not needed any more' should have been 'that's all for the moment'. I made a mental note that for the rest of this Nureyev Festival I would have to have eyes in the back of my head, be everywhere at all times and woe betide me if I ever left the stage.

We managed to gather in a few stragglers who were very disgruntled that they had not managed to escape into the sunshine and an afternoon off. Three of us started to move windmills, carts and 'mountains'. Suddenly, there was Nureyev, pushing the windmill offstage with us, helping us, really putting his shoulder to it, in order that we could proceed with the rehearsal. I don't know many performers who would have done that.

There was a brief rehearsal of the grand pas de deux from the penultimate scene. I had never watched a full-length ballet from the wings before and it was wonderful to watch people a few feet away, to see the exertion and the concentration that went into the performance from such close quarters.

I was thinking what fun this season was going to be when I was suddenly surrounded by smiling friendly matadors and bridesmaids, the corps de ballet and soloists ready for the finale. This finale made me smile with its clicking fingers and party feel, which is the cue for the curtain to come in. There was a quick exchange of words from Rudolf to the conductor and then he was gone.

Everyone seemed to breathe again. I was intrigued by the dynamics that I'd just witnessed and settled back into the prompt corner to watch the rest of the rehearsal – a reprise of any sections without Nureyev. I turned as I heard footsteps coming down the wings towards me. Nureyev. He checked with me the time of the evening performance and waved goodbye with a smile.

I learned in the days to follow that his usual routine comprised almost 12 hours of dance in one form or another and was not surprised to find him at warm-up that evening with the rest of the company. But then when they had all left, he returned to do his own work, alone, the silent controlled and controlling routine I had just witnessed for the first time.

The rehearsal was over. I was now in my own time limbo with not enough time to do anything constructive. I gathered together my motley assortment of possessions, music score, handbag and torch, and headed for the office.

The long, narrow stage management office is a shock after the rehearsals on stage. Quiet, unwelcoming. It is strange being here by myself, without the usual gaggle of stage managers working on an opera together, usually three or four of us. I am here on the Nureyev Festival all alone. I wonder if it is going to be a lonely experience, or if there are friends to be made. After a quick time check, I start the long process of deciding what to wear. I choose a Laura Ashley lightweight, pale-blue summer frock, even though it will elicit the usual remarks from the crew that, 'you can see right through that'. Evening dress for stage managers is a house rule: it makes us easier to spot in the middle of Napoleon's army standing in the wings for operas such as *War and Peace*.

The stage manager is responsible for starting the show, making sure that it all happens at the right time – from lighting and sound cues to interval times and a whole lot more that you learn over the years. Crucially, we also ensure that everyone is in the theatre and ready to perform.

On my return to the prompt corner, it is suddenly flooded with brilliant artificial sunshine, which fills the stage and sends shafts of light cutting into the wings.

Ian, one of the prompt-side crew (the prompt side being the left-hand side of the stage) walks past and says sardonically, 'Good heavens, lights! We must be about do a show!' A nightly comment.

The drapes and hangings are now in, and two large scenic houses have been rolled into position, benches and tables set in front of them, and the stage is full of dancers, ballerinas en pointe but with leg-warmers casually round their ankles and the boys from the corps de ballet practising jetés one after another, landing with resounding thumps.

I call the 'quarter', 20 minutes to curtain up, and then wander across the stage, checking the floor cloth for creases, lumps, bumps, petals and other potential death traps for dancers. I say hello to the crew on the prompt side. We talk about the dry-ice machines that are gurgling in readiness, their vast grey pipes hidden behind the masking flats, ready to create mist and atmosphere. I hunt for the small cue light boxes, with their red and green lights that signal to the crew when to move scenery or to operate dry ice or smoke, and check that the crewman responsible has seen where the cue light is and knows how long they have before they are needed.

A wonderful cacophony of sound blares out from the speakers: the sounds of a full house coming in and settling down, an orchestra waiting to tune and practising what sounds like five different ballets at the same time.

I feel the adrenalin rush through me, a Pavlovian response to the sounds, but this time I'm more excited than ever before. It is a skin-tingling, hairs-on-the-back-of-the-neck anticipation, a desperate need to see again the skills performed by a dancer in old battered shoes and a fraying knitted jumpsuit. This time it will be in costume, in front of an audience, and, this time, I know it will be the most extraordinary show of my entire life.

I also have a new job that I've never had to do backstage before. Crowd control. Not of the cast but of visitors. On this first night, there are hordes of visitors, guests and friends asking to watch from the wings. Some have managed to run the gauntlet of our fearsome stage doorkeepers, Ralph, Ben and 'little Terry', without being spotted, which is no mean feat.

I discover in the midst of this madness that one of the perks of my job is to briefly chaperone groups of stunning young men who come down the wings hesitantly each night, looking as though they have stepped straight out of *Brideshead Revisited.* They are all dressed uniformly in long pale cashmere coats and white evening scarves. They are suntanned, blond and gorgeous.

'Are you Miss Caroline?'

'Hello, yes I am,' I sigh. I shall get used to being called Caroline instead of Carolyn and I can forgive this little group anything.

'Mr Nureyev says that we have to ask you where we can stand to watch the performance.'

'How many are there of you, if you see what I mean?'

'Six, is that all right?'

Who could refuse?

The wings of a theatre are difficult to work in, with supporting braces sticking out from behind the flats with weights on them, people making exits and entrances, furniture and scenery with attendant crew moving quickly. They can also be very dark, with dry-ice machines dangerously camouflaged by the gloom, cables and now male models, beautiful ones at that. I put the little group down left in the first bay and hope that I haven't forgotten some mass exodus of 40 dancers into that 4 ft by 6 ft space during Act 1 – that would result in a pile-up and much embarrassment or even injury.

I stroll back across the stage, incongruous at 5 ft 10 in. tall in my blue cotton frock, towering over the delicate performers on stage.

I call the 'five', ten minutes to curtain up, and settle down at the desk, now brilliantly lit by the CCTV monitor with a choice of view of either the stage or conductor and a battery of cue lights and microphones. I call 'Beginners', which this time really is five minutes to curtain up. I press the first bar bell, for three minutes to go. The Coliseum is such a large theatre that double time is allowed to get people from the bars and into their seats.

At precisely three minutes to curtain up, the conductor, André Presser arrives. He is difficult to miss in immaculate white tie and tails. One of the crew says, 'Great, the wine waiter is here, we can order.' André laughs indulgently at this oft-repeated joke. He is in a no-win situation. Had he chosen to wear a white tuxedo, they would only have asked him for an ice cream.

He offers me his baton and a job swap for the evening.

'Sure, why not? You don't do very much anyway do you? Just wave your arms around. The band does their own thing. They only need you to tell them when the dancers are on stage and ready, and maybe the wardrobes [the double basses] can do that,' I joke.

He gasps in feigned horror and astonishment. 'All these years learning my art and . . .' He pretends to collapse in shock.

'No, it is a really good idea. I will be further away from Rudolf and you can deal with everything. You can handle the scene changes, can't you? Rudolf can give you notes at close quarters.'

'No, on second thoughts maybe I am safer in the pit. There is a nice big gap between him and me. We will swap tomorrow night.'

The orchestra is tuning, and the excited hum of the audience is infecting everyone. Even me. There are 2,232 people in the auditorium, waiting to see the world's greatest ballet dancer. A full house, as always, for Nureyev.

The theatre manager comes round to tell me that we have clearance, that everyone is seated and waiting. I check with the visiting ballet company that they are happy and ready to go, ready in the wings in a flurry of extravagantly embroidered tutus and nervous stretching. The crew are standing by. But one vital element is missing.

Nureyev.

After three minutes, I sense the audience is becoming restive. The expectant hush which precedes curtain up is giving way to the mumble of voices. I glance at my watch. We're five minutes late already. A lone slow handclap starts. I am surprised but think that maybe this is an ardent fan who knows from past experience how long this preamble can take before their idol appears on stage to entertain them.

A gaggle of men stand by the pass door, also glancing at their watches. They are the conductor, the theatre manager, the front-of-house manager and the promoter's representative. They're muttering nervously to each other, then turn to look at me, waiting to see what I will do, concerned that we are obviously going to be late 'up'.

'Don't worry, guys. I'll do this, this is woman's work!' I tell them. Facetiousness always comes quickly to me when under duress.

I'm used to the stars, no matter how huge their egos, standing by ready in the wings at the first bar bell, waiting to show what they can do and to receive the applause that they crave. But this would appear to be a different animal, one that hides in his dressing-room and apparently needs coaxing out on to the stage.

'Go on, sort him out, I want to get home early tonight,' one of the crew members shouts to me as I walk up the wings to the star's dressing-room, while others add their own ribald comments. I discover later that they've seen many stage managers try this. I have no idea what's in store for me.

My footsteps up the wings are now accompanied by a slow crescendo in the handclapping. Two thousand pairs of hands are demanding satisfaction. The ballet dancers are warmed up and quickly cooling down, the orchestra is tuned and raring to go, the conductor is ready to start, the promoter is fretting, but there is no sign of the star of the show.

As I arrive outside the dressing-room, I take a deep breath. I am nervous.

I knock. There is no reply.

The audience has taken up the chant, 'Why are we waiting?' in full-throated roar. It is incredible. I have never heard a sound like it. It feels more like the real Roman Colosseum than St Martin's Lane. I have never heard a ballet or opera audience sound so threatening. I now understand that they had practised this many times over the years, but to me at that moment, it was extraordinary.

I knock again, say my name, more stridently than I would have liked, and begin to enter carefully.

And there he is.

His arms are stretched out, questioning me. He is standing back-lit in the glare of bare make-up light bulbs and a bright white Formica-trimmed dressing table.

He is stark naked.

At first I am embarrassed that I have disturbed him, then angry. Why didn't he stop me from coming in? But he knew that I would come in; and then I realise that I am being challenged, he wants to shock me. It is deliberate.

And I take it all in, this living, breathing version of Michelangelo's *David*.

I am stunned. Speechless certainly, but somehow not shocked. It would be difficult to be shocked by such beauty.

It is impossible not to look at all of him, to take it all in and I know that this is exactly what I am meant to do.

He is slightly shorter than me. His skin is pale, almost luminous. It is the most beautiful body that I have ever seen. He is broad chested, every muscle defined, carved, worked, tuned, with a slim waist. His arms are muscular, elegant and end in sinewy shoulders. The fact that he is male is not in question. There can be no doubt.

He has huge thighs in comparison to his slim waist, and large calves that end in knotted, dry-skinned, wide, peasant-like feet. His big toes curl inward to rest on the other toes.

There is not one inch of him that is not built for purpose, for work and for looking at.

I return to his face, and that wide sensuous mouth, the intriguing scar that only exaggerates his beauty, the superb cheekbones and challenging eyes. He has carefully brushed his golden wispy hair back and it is heavily sprayed into place.

I am still experiencing a confused mixture of anger and embarrassment. I would never walk in on someone uninvited and I am angry that I have been put in this unprofessional position.

'I am so sorry,' I stutter. 'I didn't realise. We are really quite late.' I am now very flustered and can feel myself starting to speak breathless gibberish.

He stares at me defiantly.

'You want me to go on like this?'

We lock eyes. Eventually, in the silence, he starts to roughly pull on his jockstrap; I notice he looks momentarily embarrassed, which is intriguing.

'I just wondered how much longer you were going to be?' I finally stammer. 'If it is much longer then I think that I will have to make an announcement to the audience.'

I wait for whatever blast is going to hit me.

'If you make an announcement, I'll go home!' This is a new form of Russian roulette.

'If you go home, then I'd have to make another announcement,' I say carefully.

We just stare at one another and I crack first.

'I'll see you on stage, then.' I back out quickly from his dressing-room and from this confrontation.

I have no idea who won that round, but I suspect neither of us did. I am zinging with adrenalin and that unexpected blast of testosterone has left me sparkle-eyed from this naked 'street fight'.

Is this what it is going to be like every night? Over 2,000 people chanting, the crew jeering and a naked Mexican stand-off with this man?

The walk back to the stage seems twice as long and very lonely. I don't even know if my tactics will work with him. What if he refuses and leaves anyway? Oh, great, terrific, wonderful. My first night and he walks. Now I feel sick. Try explaining that one away. 'We were late, so I went to see him, he was naked.' It does not bear thinking about.

Now I'm not sure whether this detached professional approach is what he wants. But I stood my ground and stood up to him, and my instincts are that this was what he wanted, not someone who ran or burst into tears, but a partner, an equal in his games, someone with the interests of the show at heart.

The crew are lined up in the wings to gauge what my reaction has been. There's some suppressed giggling from those who knew exactly what was waiting for me behind that shut door.

'All right, Carolyn? Bet you didn't need a magnifying glass and tweezers then!'

I know I am blushing deeply from anger and embarrassment.

There is hysterical laughing. I didn't need any help in seeing what I was meant to see. I take a deep breath and wait.

So, now I have met Rudolf Nureyev, all of him. My experience a world away from that of the crowd just a few feet on the other side of the curtain who are still chanting and wondering when, if ever, we are going to start the show.

The doors upstage swing open and here he comes with dresser in attendance. Glaring. Looking at no one, focused.

The conductor waves at me. I call out, 'Break a leg' to him as a good-luck wish and he goes down to the pit. When I judge that he is halfway down the two narrow sets of stairs, I push the house lights button to down, ready for André to take his bow, and there is polite, slightly shamefaced applause, as we lose the football stadium crowd with their jeering and clapping, and the polite, refined ballet audience returns. I stand by to take up the curtain and watch the monitor in the prompt-corner desk as the overture starts.

I call quietly to the dancers on stage to, 'Stand by, please,' and pull the lever of the curtain towards me. Scene one of *Don Quixote*, the marketplace, full of action and colour, is revealed to the audience and we have started the first performance.

We start what will become a very 'standard' 15 minutes late, very un-British and it feels very unprofessional. I sit at the prompt corner and start to write out the time sheet: 7.46. It will always be 7.46, never 7.30 and for the first time I wonder what to write as reason for the late start. 'Stroppy Russian giving me a hard time' might be an option.

I look up as Rudolf Nureyev walks down the wings ready to make his way to his first entrance as the barber, Basilio. He stares me out, kicks off his clogs and focuses hard on the stage. There is a frisson down the wings as dancers look but try not to catch his eye as he prepares to enter. I talk to the follow-spot operator over the headsets to tell him to stand by to pick up Nureyev mid-stage right. I finally announce to the dressing-rooms the end of the delay, 'Curtain up Act 1, ladies and gentlemen,' and settle back, ready to let the music and sights envelop me.

The first night of the season and my first night with Nureyev. It is like 'trying to join an express train', to quote the actor Nigel Stock. He used to say that if you joined a show halfway through its run, then everyone else is having an easy stroll round the stage and you're running along the edges trying to get them to stop so that you can join in. It is like being in two totally different productions. Everyone else has rehearsed and performed for months. I have had one day compared to the weeks that Zurich Ballet have been rehearsing and performing on tour.

After my years with English National Opera, ballet has come as a surprise. Sometimes there are no music scores; you just have to learn when the cues happen. You have to rely on expert knowledge gleaned over the years and understand the 'in' references to various set pieces and sections. I had not managed to absorb very much at all in my one day.

But just now, Rudolf Nureyev is ready to do what he was born to do and what everyone wants to see.

He stands upstage centre and the world stops. He just stands. That's all. You can see everyone in the wings look and say to themselves, 'How does he do that?' There are 50 people on stage but he is the only one that you notice. And so, of course, do about half a dozen amateur photographers in the audience, desperate for a memento of their idol. This is very distracting for any performer, let alone a dancer. Alerted to their location by the guys in the lighting box at the back of the stalls, we start what will be a daily 'seek, explain and if necessary grab camera ever so nicely' by the front-of-house staff.

There is a flurry of activity in the wings and I look to see two nervous dressers standing by as Rudolf exits. A quick change occurs, into hat and cloak, right there, with Rudolf dripping sweat and mopping his brow with piles of tissues.

He walks down towards me to re-enter and says to me quickly, 'Make announcement – no flash photography.'

'Of course!' I reply, as he makes another entrance. His bravura solo produces cheers and shouts of 'Bravo!' It is a good night and he has astounded everyone. The Nureyev of myth and legend is with us tonight, not Old Galoshes. He walks downstage to acknowledge the applause to left and right, then waits for Yoko, who is playing Kitri, his love, to join him, inviting her onto his stage and into his presence. The pas de deux that follows is a joy and is rewarded by thunderous applause.

Rudolf exits and as he is drying his face with handfuls of tissues that are dropped in a pile on the floor, he shouts at me, 'Stop the photography or I don't dance!' So, no pressure there, then. I get the first full hit of the flared nostrils. All the visiting company, guests and watchers look at me, waiting for me to do something, so I hassle the much beleaguered front-of-house manager by phone, though he is already out on patrol trying to find the culprits who have managed to ignore every single notice about photography.

As we were so late starting, I wonder what our intervals are going to be like. I'm pleasantly surprised. They're short, there are no delays, no waiting for Rudolf. His body has been switched on and it takes over. But we do make the promised announcement about flash photography. A very prim round of applause greets this announcement. You can almost hear sanctimonious tutting. 'As if any of us would do something like that! Well really.'

The show is going well, people come running off past me, smiling and waving. One dancer stops to say hello.

He's tall and handsome with a mass of bubble curls and a huge smile. I learn later in the interval from the visiting crew that this is Robert Tracy, Nureyev's partner. He smiles, waves and goes on stage. He looks so warm and approachable that I know that we are going to be friends. There is an aura of gentleness and humour about him. I now have someone else to watch and he, too, really can dance.

There are groups of people watching in the wings, staring out from the dark on to the brilliantly lit stage – crew, dancers and friends, exactly what I would expect for the first night of a major show. I can see Rudolf staring into the wings when he is walking around the stage, looking suspiciously at all the people. He's always suspicious, always watching. His eyes are never still.

Rudolf again exits to the prompt corner and shouts at me that the conductor is going too fast and that I must go and tell him. 'It should be one two three then dah dah dah!' he screams, beating time to me so that I understand. I understand the musical request but have no idea what to do. This is not an easy task. I hesitate, wondering whether to phone the conductor and hope that he can get the phone – after all he is conducting at the moment – or do I go down to the pit, trawl through the fiddles and try and tell him that way? Luckily, by the time I have finished dithering, the section is over, but I feel as if I have failed. Was I really meant to do anything or just support him in agreement? Nureyev doesn't mention it again.

We are now reaching the end of the final act and I check to see that I have enough staff to help me with the curtain calls and volunteers from the ushers to present flowers. Following the full stage curtain calls and pulling the house curtain in and out whilst shouting, 'Everyone forward. Everyone back. Conductor now please', we rush on to pull back the huge section of the curtain with handles, allowing the dancers to go through for their solo and paired calls and to receive their flowers.

So this is what it is all about.

An incredible night of tangible passion and inspiration. Screams, shouts and hundreds of flowers hurled at the forestage for one person, Nureyev. This goes on and on for 30 minutes. It is an extraordinary experience – the noise, the heavy scents of the flowers, his apparent reluctance to go back on and do another call. Then that solo call that Rudolf has made his trademark: his right arm in the air and looking right to left and then up to the balcony. Smiling all the while roses are hurled at his feet, hundreds of them, continuously. Rudolf's dresser waits patiently beside me behind the curtain, holding his towel, clogs and tissues. I have never seen anything in my working life like this adulation.

'Every night it will be like this, you wait,' says Terry, one of the props staff, whilst standing at an interesting angle, leaning backwards, like a yachtsman on a serious starboard tack, holding one part of the huge curtain. 'Every night, hours of it, complete madness, and you wait until you try and get out of the stage door, it takes hours!' I don't care. I am completely and utterly hooked and on a Nureyev-induced high.

Various members of the crew and dressers are standing in their coats waiting to see how long this will continue and anxiously glancing at their watches with concern for last trains and buses. The pass door opens as various VIPs and friends are ushered through by security to wait, looking slightly ill at ease in their evening dress in this working environment, clutching their programmes and coats.

The clapping finally starts to calm and when I check with Rudolf, he waves his arm, other hand on hip and turns away to signal enough. We close the curtain.

I turn round expecting an empty stage and I am surprised to find the full company waiting behind us, along with Dame Ninette de Valois from the Royal Ballet and the directors of Zurich Ballet. They would like to take a full company photograph with Rudolf, they say.

There is panic as we try to get the full stage lighting up, terrified that we might fail and this moment be lost for ever. The lighting staff may have left already but luckily we catch them just in time. Though disgruntled, they are coerced back into their control box. The lights on stage come back up. People are placed and huddled together – Rudolf in the centre and Dame Ninette to his right, Yoko Morishita on her right.

I have never seen such a happy group of people: not staged, nor posed, but real joy.

Towards the end of the week I ask Rudolf if he would sign a copy of the photo for me. This isn't easy to do. As a professional you aren't meant to autograph hunt, it just isn't done. But this feels different. With a huge smile and not a sigh in sight he does so. Wonderful. I feel that if I never work with him again, I now have something to remember him by. Just like one of the thousands of fans waiting to see him.

The company disperses slowly, laughing, waving goodnight to me and the remaining crew. We are all smiling, even the crew. It is almost difficult to leave now and lose this moment. Rudolf walks away, carefully assisting Dame Ninette over cables and jutting corners of scenery. The guests who have waited in the wings during this scene will now have to wait outside his dressing-room, hovering, lurking, as he showers and changes.

We bring up the working lights in the auditorium and wait a little while before kicking the tabs forward to pull in the hundreds of flowers that are lying on the forestage or apron. By tradition these get distributed amongst the crew, dressers and friends. Even so, it is sad to find decaying ones the next morning that we haven't grabbed, left to wither and die on the extremities of the stage and in the depths of the orchestra pit.

The wings are empty and the crew are almost running up the wings, clutching armfuls of roses, with the goal of a quick pint or their bus home. It is now nearly 40 minutes since the end of the performance proper. We are back in our cold, grey, working-light world. The magic has ended.

In the office I sit down to type up the show report: our running times, intervals and the length of the curtain calls. An essential final part of the show, where overtime is scrutinised, delays questioned and sometimes, though thankfully rarely, accidents are noted by theatre management and promoters. With a huge old typewriter, lots of Tippex, battling with carbon paper, counting the minutes, this takes me some time. I then change into my everyday clothes and wonder fleetingly which frock will do for the next evening. I am relieved that it is the end of a very long couple of days, but I am excited and looking forward to the rest of the season, despite the silent battle with a nude superstar.

I walk through the swing doors, up the stairs and along to the stage door, where I find the star of the show already showered, changed and sitting in the stage doorkeeper's rather shabby little office. He is framed by the half stable door as he perches on a really ancient stool, which I know is ripped and has foam stuffing sticking out. He is signing autograph after autograph in precious books and on framed photographs lovingly produced from plastic carrier bags, doing his duty to his fans. He's not exactly smiling as he accepts rose after rose from adoring women. 'Always the women never the men,' he once told me, laughing ruefully. A thoroughly bored Ben, the stage doorkeeper left on late duty, is propping up the wall, watching disinterestedly.

Out in Bedfordbury, the street behind the Coliseum, there are hundreds of people, all waiting to catch a glimpse of their idol. I have never seen anything like it. Some fans rush past me ecstatic. 'Isn't this wonderful? It is just like the old days!'

It is a balmy summer's night, warm and special. Then there's a throaty roar from a car's engine as Rudolf and entourage try to manoeuvre through the throngs in his brown TR4 along Bedfordbury to New Row, but it is a difficult process with fans chasing and cameras snapping all the time.

I start my journey home through the throngs of the Strand, down Villiers Street and over the spooky, narrow footbridge over the Thames, Hungerford Bridge, past all the buskers and beggars to Waterloo Station.

Later, on the train going home to the outer suburbs of London, I look at all the people with their Nureyev programmes and muse over the two different performances we have seen that night. Grinning inanely to myself, I remember the story of how hotel staff are trained. If they walk into a room and find someone there undressed, then they are taught to say 'Excuse me, sir' for a lady and vice versa in an attempt to reassure the guest that their secrets are safe, nothing has really been seen. I picture what I really have just seen and say to myself that there is no way I would have been able to get that vision wrong.

That thought, and the memories of the wonderful dancing, keep me going throughout the long train journey home.

CHAPTER ONE

Rewriting History

1980 was a fantastic summer. Night after night of wonderful ballet, ecstatic crowds and those endless curtain calls. At the end of the season, I went back to my job-hunting, looking for work as an itinerant company or stage manager.

I didn't know then that 1980 was going to be the first of a run of seasons with the Nureyev Festivals, not only in London but also in Manchester. I was going to get a lot more experience of Nureyev and the 'announcement' spats before curtain up, and I was going to learn about this extraordinary man's sense of humour, his love of art and architecture and his dedication to his work.

I have been very lucky to work with many amazing people throughout my career, but over the years, the memories of the times that I worked with the man everyone called 'Rudi' stand out.

I had seen the pictures of this glamorous young man who took the world by storm first by defecting, then by dancing. He was not a spy, a businessman or somebody who had hidden behind the walls of academia. He was 'just a ballet dancer'. But I am not aware of another defection gaining such publicity at that time, especially from East to West. It gave him huge cachet before many of us had even seen him dance. And to add to this glamour, he was young and insanely beautiful.

We were to learn the many complex reasons for his escape at Le Bourget airport in Paris. He was on tour with the Kirov at the time and had heard rumours that he was to be sent home. When he arrived at the airport to catch a flight to London with the other members of the company, he saw the 'men in suits' hovering around the terminal. He had made a lot of friends in Paris and although he was not alone in his night-time excursions into the city, he was the one that 'they' were watching most closely, the one that was causing them the most anxiety. He was told that like everyone else he was going back to Russia, but he alone was to have the honour of dancing for Krushchev. Although they said that after the gala he would of course eventually be joining the Kirov when they moved on to London, Rudolf didn't believe them. He knew that this was going to be no honour at all, and was just a way of getting him back to Russia, away from his new-found French friends and back home where, apart from his behaviour, his emerging homosexuality would be questioned and his future would be bleak. The combination of this and the prospect of being sent back to dance with a provincial company in Ufa, to tour endlessly or perhaps, if he was lucky, to dance 15 performances a year with the Kirov, was anathema to him. He made a split-second life-changing decision. Hiding behind pillars in the airport's terminal to dodge the two KGB men, he 'surrendered' himself to the French police and asked for their help. With no luggage and only the clothes he was wearing, it must have been a momentous decision to leave behind his family, his friends and his culture. For many years after this he spent his life on the road travelling as a temporary Austrian citizen.

Rudi had seen foreign companies on tour in Russia and knew their standards and the possibilities that were there for him. Crucially, he had seen Erik Bruhn dance in videos and watched the man who was, until Rudolf's defection, the greatest ballet star in the world.

After his defection, Nureyev joined the Marquis de Cuevas Ballet in Paris and the rumours about this extraordinary dancer began to circulate. His performance of the famous Bluebird solo in *The Sleeping Beauty* astounded the critics. The stories of Nureyev's ability spread round the world.

The ballet dancer Maria Tallchief, an ex-lover of Erik Bruhn's, introduced Nureyev to Bruhn. Rudolf travelled to Denmark to watch Tallchief perform in a special gala and then stayed on to train with Bruhn. During their daily class together, Nureyev began to learn and absorb the Western style of classical ballet and a relationship began to form between the two men. Rudolf was 23 years old and Bruhn was 10 years older. Bruhn had the body that Nureyev craved and they both sought perfection in their dancing, but the 'marriage' of Nureyev and Bruhn was to rock Erik's already shaky confidence in his own ability.

Rudolf begged Erik to teach him everything, but then towards the end of Erik's life accused him at a dinner party, in front of a crowd of friends, of never having taught him 'to pirouette properly'. Rudolf was jealous of the reviews that Erik received and in turn Erik was overshadowed by the press and publicity that Rudolf received. There were numerous stories of their heavy drinking, and Bruhn was a heavy smoker.

There could be no doubt about their affection for one another, however. When he heard that Erik was very ill, Rudolf flew to his bedside in Toronto, where Erik had been director of National Ballet of Canada. Erik died of lung cancer on 1 April 1986, but there was speculation that he had been suffering from Aids.

Whilst Rudolf was training in Denmark, he was invited by Margot Fonteyn to dance at her gala at the Royal Opera House on 21 February 1961, in aid of the Royal Academy of Dance (RAD), and the reviews applauded him. The Nureyev phenomenon had come to England.

Dame Ninette de Valois asked the 23-year-old Rudolf to partner the 42-year-old Margot Fonteyn for just three performances of *Giselle* and the legendary Fonteyn and Nureyev stage partnership was born.

The world watched in amazement, devouring every single little piece of news about Nureyev and Fonteyn. This relationship captured the public's imagination, not only because of their appearances on stage but also at parties, opening nights and clubs all round the world. People were enchanted with the renewed career of Britain's prima ballerina and her partnership with this young Russian. Everyone watched them dance together and just thought it impossible that two people could show such passion and completeness on stage if they were not together off stage as well.

Nureyev's explanation was, 'It's not me, it's not her, it's the sameness of the goal.'

Rumours were spreading throughout the theatre world not only about the ambiguity of this relationship with Margot Fonteyn but also about Nureyev's sexual excesses and his temper. He appeared daily in all the newspapers, either with Fonteyn or, as I later discovered, just because he smiled one day on stage. This was a new type of superstar, not a rock or movie star but a classical ballet dancer.

He must have increased the popularity of ballet a hundredfold, transforming its image from being a nice middle-class pursuit of the arts to something accessible, with a 'glamour boy' to go and see. In the swinging '60s of London, Nureyev was everywhere, and he joined the ranks of the other icons of the time: Brigitte Bardot, Elvis Presley, Peter O'Toole, The Beatles, Sean Connery, Marilyn Monroe and all the rising stars.

On the artistic and creative side, no one could doubt that there was a new vital power on the ballet scene. The reports about Rudolf's dancing enthused that he 'flew', he was 'animal-like' and took 'risks' on stage. After his Royal Ballet debut in 1962 with Margot Fonteyn in *Giselle*, he choreographed *La Bayadère, Raymonda*, *Swan Lake, The Sleeping Beauty*, *Don Quixote, Tancredi*, *The Nutcracker*, *Romeo and Juliet, Manfred*, *The Tempest, Bach Suite*, *Washington Square* and *Cinderella*, and performed all over the world. Numerous roles were created for him and the whole ballet repertoire had the Nureyev stamp on it. He was probably the first classical ballet dancer who also successfully performed in modern dance and he changed the role of the male dancer for ever. Before Nureyev, male dancers had traditionally been just the 'chevalier' to the ballerina, an escort and support for her. Now he created huge demanding solos for himself that were to live on for the next 30 years and set new standards of achievement for dancers all over the world. He was a workaholic who never stopped dancing, who never wanted to stop dancing.

He directed the film version of *Don Quixote* with Australian Ballet in 1972, and in the late '70s he appeared as Valentino in Ken Russell's movie of the same name to mixed reviews. Then, to prove what a showman and consummate performer he was, he reached out to millions of people in their own homes, appearing on television in

1977 in *The Muppet Show* as Miss Piggy's partner in 'Swine Lake'; as a grand finale he performed a Fred Astaire tap-dancing routine in top hat and tails, 'shooting' Muppets with his cane as he spun.

It was an extraordinary transformation for the only boy of four children, born into a desperately poor family in Ufa. His mother chose the name of Rudolf because she liked the sound of it. This love of words and their musicality was passed on to her son and explains his sometimes strange choice of language: for example, the use of 'Galoshes' because the word had such a satisfying sound.

His father was determined that his only son was to become a doctor or an engineer, but Rudi, aged six, had been smuggled into a theatre on New Year's Eve by his mother, hidden under her coat, to see a ballet company perform and had become transfixed by the dancing and even the gaudy stage curtain. From that night on he knew that he had to become a dancer.

When I read about this early life, when Rudolf was sent to school wearing his sisters' clothes and with no shoes, how they had no bathroom and all lived in one room, I was, and still am, amazed at the fragile links and circumstances that ended with Nureyev dancing as a major star in the West. He showed incredible strength and courage in his desire to be a dancer, a tenacity that first took him to Leningrad and to the Kirov. Considered by his classmates at 17 years old to be an 'oaf', a peasant, he ran the gauntlet of authority, going out at night to sneak in to watch performances in the theatre rather than staying safely tucked up in the dormitory. He was years older than his fellow students and a late starter. He also committed the worst sin of all: he was better than everyone else. His mentor and teacher Alexander Pushkin ignored him at first, almost made him prove his worth, then agreed to Nureyev moving into his class and to teaching this unique young man. This strength of spirit and belief in his own ability enabled Nureyev to surmount the various hurdles or challenges that stood in his way, and eventually gave him the courage to defect that day in Paris.

When I met him in 1980, he was 42 years old, an age when most ballet dancers have long since retired. They have accepted that the walk-on role of the character actor/dancer is their lot for as long as they are fit and willing, and are not destined to become artistic directors or choreographers. But Rudi was still taking on the leading roles and performing over 200 times a year.

For me, as for everyone who knew him, Rudi's death in 1993 was an incredible blow. I greedily bought all the books that came out about him over the ensuing years and devoured them, trying to find out more about this person I had worked with. I wanted to know if people had seen what I had seen, had the same conversations, and I wanted to know more about the private Nureyev.

Despite the many tomes about Rudolf that appeared, factual and some not so factual, I knew from my work with the Nureyev Festivals at the London Coliseum and later in Manchester that there were people who had never told their stories of this icon. I wanted to share these stories and I also knew that an account of life backstage in a theatre, the touring tales that theatre folk all have and the added glamour of Rudolf Nureyev would be an alluring combination. I wanted to show people what this whole experience had been like by writing what everyone started calling a 'memoir'. This sounded a little grand to me, but it was not going to be a chronological biography, written by a balletomane. It would instead be my memories as a stage manager, a workmate. It would be the account of my time spent working with and speaking to Nureyev, observing him over a period of six years. Perhaps this was my way of helping to keep Rudolf's memory alive, of reminding people what this man was like, who might as well have announced his arrival from Atlantis, the impact he had on the world at the time.

In 2002, almost ten years after Rudolf's death, my quest started with a conscious effort to find Robert Tracy, Rudolf's partner and friend. I was sad that we had drifted apart and I wanted to ask him everything that I had never had the chance to ask at the time. I wanted to know what it was like to live with this man, how they had met and what had eventually prompted Robert to sue his lover and friend of some 14 years.

I found two more people who also knew and loved Rudi: Bill Akers and Roger Myers. Their story starts in 1962 in Australia and spans nearly 30 years to the last harrowing weeks at the end of 1992 in Paris.

I spoke to Yoko Morishita, prima ballerina with Matsuyama Ballet in Tokyo, who partnered Rudi for years with many companies, and learned from her what it was actually like to dance on stage with this man and to learn from him.

During conversations about writing this book, and from chance encounters and comments to friends all over the world, I was to discover many more people with their own stories of meeting their hero, from waiters to hairdressers, designers to A-list celebrities. Most of these were accounts of brief sightings, but they all wanted to say that they had known Nureyev. He still has that power, to make people yearn for association, 11 years after his death.

With my cast assembled, I was ready to find out more about Nureyev's temper, his obsessions, the women in his life and his day-to-day routine, which included his nightly 'hunting' or cruising.

Nureyev came with a reputation for impossible tantrums, an uncontrollable temper and generally being 'difficult'. I had first-hand experience of the tantrums and moods, and had watched the different dynamics on stage that could change in a split second. In retrospect, I am stunned that I went through that naked stand-off routine and the obligatory row about announcements. This couldn't have happened every single night but it seemed to stick in my memory as a mandatory occurrence, a ritual to fire him up every night that we performed *Swan Lake*, *Giselle* or *Don Quixote*. I was to discover, whilst writing this book, that the challenge of people's memories, including my own, was to be the greatest hurdle. We had all rather got into the habit of saying, 'He was impossible.' I remember telling a theatre director on a production at the Old Vic that he was 'as difficult as Nureyev' to deal with. I think he was quite flattered. But, when he asked me to recount any really bad incidents, even then in '86, I couldn't really recall any specifically vile moments. Perhaps it had all become relative and I had found some super-strength rose-tinted spectacles. But I did remember that Rudi was also very funny and part of my nightly entertainment was to ask him if he wanted anything from the canteen, purely to see the look of horror on his face. I never expected him to rise to the challenge of the culinary delights of the infamous under-stage canteen but it made me laugh and he indulged me.

Robert Tracy was an obvious but intriguing source for the answers to some of my questions. He had first-hand experience of living and working with this icon. They had started out as lovers and after a huge row and time apart, they moved in together again, but as friends.

Fourteen years later, when Rudolf was very ill and drawing up his will, Robert sued his friend for more money. Rudolf was going to leave Robert just £500 a month in his will. Prevented from seeing his friend to discuss the matter, it was some ten years later that Robert discovered that Rudolf had wanted to settle out of court. I had read about the reactions from some of Nureyev's friends to this lawsuit for palimony and about their feeling that Robert was trying to take over Nureyev's Dakota Building apartment, apparently refusing to move. Although Robert had some staunch supporters, there appeared to be a faction who basically disowned him, who did not understand how he could sue his friend. These were some of the people who thought of him as a hanger-on, a leech who never paid for anything. As Robert was a student, I wasn't sure how he was meant to contribute to the amazing lifestyle that they shared but I wanted to hear Robert's story for myself, as I was surprised that a friend and lover would sue someone he had been with for so long. I needed to understand what would prompt someone to do this, to take such tough action. It sounded like the final resort after a very acrimonious split-up, not the accepted behaviour or 'done thing' when one half of the partnership or friendship is dying. After all, he must have known the effect it would have on the friends and observers, who perhaps, like me, didn't have all the facts. I was to learn that it was purely about survival, not malice or pique.

I was haunted by one particular vision of Robert. It was 1983. He was standing on the pavement outside the ballet company's hotel in Manchester. He had his hands in his pockets, standing alone, white T-shirt, cotton trousers, bag slung over his shoulder, his wonderful bubbly hair, greeting me with a huge smile. It was a really hot day. He was standing amidst the usual chaos of lost souls from the ballet company waiting for instructions after a long journey, disgorged from a coach, bleary eyed and staring at the surroundings. It was a compelling image of happy times.

But discovering Robert's current whereabouts was by no means easy. After all these years, I had lost contact with him. Even if I succeeded in finding him, would he remember me or want to talk to me? I had no way of knowing.

I hated the job I was doing in the late 1990s. I was definitely not put on this planet to work in a tiny grey office that resembled a stationery cupboard, removed from the front line of shows and unable to do the things that I loved. As head of production for a large events company, there was no music coming from the stage; in fact, there was no stage to wander down to and check. The shows were car launches, exhibitions and sales meetings, with gala dinners, cabarets or horrendous discos at the end, not fabulous ballets or operas, and whilst I loved the people I was working with, the people I worked for were far removed from the theatre folk that I had worked with for years. I was stifled and I felt trapped. My search for Robert became a way of keeping the 'theatrical luvvie', the real me and my soul, alive.

Day after day I would try various paths on the then less-sophisticated Internet, but it was not producing anything that helped me. I began to feel that I was on a fool's errand, especially when the umpteenth letter came back to me with 'unknown' written all over it. I told myself to get over it and the search for Robert stopped for a while. Perhaps it was simply not meant to be. In all likelihood, Robert wouldn't remember me if we did speak or meet. He might even be dead.

And then, in late November 2002, while reading through one of the biographies on Rudi again, I stopped at the passage mentioning Violette Verdy. Violette was an ex-prima ballerina with New York City Ballet. She had been the artistic director of Boston Ballet and of Paris Opéra Ballet. She was a good friend to Rudolf and Robert for many years. In 1980, she had reunited Rudolf and Robert after their falling out, and now she was about to perform the same good turn for me, too.

I was thrilled to find her on the web. Even though I didn't know her well, I took a chance and fired off an e-mail into the ether, to the university where she is professor of ballet. I told her that we might have met with Boston Ballet, but I was not sure and anyway, this was years later, she had no reason to remember me even if we had met. I explained that I was sad that I had lost touch with Robert, embarrassed that I had not tried to contact him when Rudi had died and that I was thinking about putting my experiences down on paper. Nothing happened. Not for days, no response, nothing. Then a polite non-committal reply arrived from a member of Violette's staff, saying that she had forwarded my message. I was feeling resigned to the prospect that this book or project was going to remain a dream and nothing more.

Then, at last, came a message from Violette herself telling me that not only did Robert remember me, but he was also looking forward to speaking to me.

So here I am, one week later, sitting on the edge of my bed in semi-darkness, the nocturnal sounds of tawny owls out hunting in the Suffolk countryside breaking through the jumble of my memories.

Spread out in front of me, in a fan shape, are six pictures of Rudi. He looks beautiful, proud and poised on the covers of the Nureyev Festival programmes. On the cover of this first programme in 1980, he is a young, beautiful Romeo from another production; in later photographs, his features become more reflective with an older, more lived-in face, but he still has that extraordinary body. The photos, programmes and letters are not the sum total of the most extraordinary six years of my life; I have the memories as well.

It is one o'clock in the morning on 12 December and it is very cold. Robert's voice sounds just the way I remember: warm, friendly and now excited, just as I am. I am relieved that he is pleased to hear from me after 18 years. In the silence of my bedroom deep in the countryside with my heart pounding in my ears, this is a moment in time to relish.

'Violette told me that you were looking for me. Well, here I am. Ten years since Rudolf died, can you believe it, ten years?'

And, magically, Robert and I take up without a pause exactly where we had left off all those years ago. This is a capacity in people which never fails to surprise me; perhaps it is particularly pronounced in the theatre world where you spend weeks or months working with someone, then don't see them again for years. No matter how many years have passed, how many times you have not sent a card on their first night, it doesn't matter. You just carry on.

'Rudolf would have been 65 this year, Carolyn – can you imagine?'

No, I can't imagine Rudolf Nureyev at 65. In my mind he will always be the powerful, beautiful man who stood next to me and called himself 'Old Galoshes'. I cannot imagine what he would look like or how impossible he would be at 65.

I ask Robert, 'So do you think that he would still have been dancing?' 'He didn't know anything else,' answers Robert. 'But what would it have been like?' There is a long pause and a feeling that we are both horrified at the thought. I remember off-nights and then finally seeing the filmed proof on video of Rudi returning to dance at the Kirov in 1987, watching a performance that had to happen for him, but probably should not have.

'Imagine if Rudolf had had children?' Robert jokes. And we laugh incredulously. Yet, as Robert says, it was a dream of Rudi's, and later I am to discover there were women who would have been very happy to help him realise this dream.

'You know,' says Robert, 'I was seven when he defected to the West.'

'In 1961?'

'Yes, right.'

I have a lot of questions. I want to know how they had met and what that must have felt like to a young dancer like Robert, to be approached and admired by this star. I wonder what their lives had been like together for those 14 years and what had not been told before. I want to hear from Robert what he knew had happened and what he knew was just 'pure fantasy'.

'I have read so much about you, Robert. Some of it sounds bizarre. Is it all true?' I ask him.

'Most people did not even bother to speak to me,' he says, 'or if they did, they did not record it and just wrote what they wanted to, anyway.' 'Rewriting history,' Robert calls it.

It is a good phrase. He sounds resigned but not a victim.

Before I start asking a long list of questions, I explain to Robert that I had always wanted to write down my experiences of working with Rudi. Robert is quick to say that he thinks it is a great idea and then adds, 'At least you knew him. It would be good, a stage manager's view, and you are asking different questions.' I understand this to mean that I don't have to start from the beginning, with the obvious questions about his temper, and the omnipresent 'What was he like?'

But asking questions about someone you both knew has other, less obvious drawbacks. It is easy for some of your questions to be brushed aside and sometimes your relationship can be used as an excuse that you should know it all anyway, so why are you asking? If I push too far or get too close, Robert pulls up the drawbridge to stop further intrusion with a quick retort: 'Come on, you know what he was like.'

It stops me absolutely dead in my tracks. It is very clever. I retreat. Yes, I did know him but I didn't eat, dance, talk shop and just live with him day after day. I knew an impossible, friendly, difficult, professional, amusing guy – a world-famous dancer who took time to trust and evaluate people. Perhaps, as a friend, I am also a little too sensitive while conducting this 'interview', and my belief that there should always be things that are private, intimate and your own memories not to be shared isn't always helpful either.

I wanted to start at the beginning with how Robert was picked by Nureyev out of all the vast numbers of potential lovers back in 1979. I knew that Robert had been selected to be one of the few dancers for a production of Balanchine's *Le Bourgeois Gentilhomme* in New York, a revival for Rudolf. Robert and Rudi met in a less than glamorous rehearsal studio.

I am sure that most people would find even the words 'rehearsal studio' glamorous. More often than not, however, these are usually just one step up in comfort and decor from a changing-room in a school sports hall. They have wooden floors and mirrors on at least two sides. But they can be cold unwelcoming places with no natural daylight, or if there is any then it invariably comes from tiny high windows that turn out on inspection to be impossible to either close or open and certainly offer no distractions or clue as to the time of day or weather. Usually there is a battered upright piano, and unforgiving plastic chairs finish the furnishings, whilst the all-pervading smell of feet and bodies seeps from every crack in the floor.

It is not exactly the most romantic of meeting places. But in New York, in 1979, this was the setting for the start of a 14-year friendship. Robert calls this period in Rudolf's life the 'downside of the ecstasy', when Rudolf was past his prime, in his 40s, but still dancing.

Robert was just 25 years old when the 41-year-old Rudi asked him out to tea. During the afternoon, Robert asked Rudolf about his tour to Egypt and they had a perfectly civilised afternoon tea – nothing else happened – and Rudolf asked Robert to call him.

Robert really did not think that Rudolf was serious about wanting him to call, after all he was a star and someone that Robert had watched from afar for years, but a few days later, Rudolf demanded to know why he had not heard from him.

Robert's voice on the phone to me some 23 years later still sounds amazed.

'It was a whirlwind, Carolyn. We were almost instantly physically attracted. I was 25, wild and open to anything. We spent the first three days in bed. Then, I just let Rudolf call the shots. I always thought that it was not going to last. I just went with it and it lasted all that time.'

I say to Robert that, had it been me, during those first few days of being with Rudolf I would have had to keep pinching myself in sheer disbelief that this incredibly beautiful man had chosen me instead of all the others. Robert sounds incredulous.

'I know, and the friendship lasted all those years.'

There is a pause in the conversation as I can feel us both visualise this man, conjuring up our own personal image of him. To me he would be standing centre stage, hand on hip, always with a slight curl of the lip, inviting the ballerina to take the stage with an expression that seemed to say, 'Go on, it is your turn now, impress me. I will let you.' Always challenging.

As a student, Robert's income was minimal, of course, about $200 a month, and there he was at the start of a life of 'helicopters, Concorde and caviar', wining and dining with princesses, the true A-list of that time, all over the world, and sharing a life with the world's greatest ballet dancer, fêted wherever they went. I can imagine the 'whirlwind' that Robert described. Listening to him, I can hear the disbelief at how his life changed so dramatically, from a student to, in his description, a 'five-star lifestyle' and he became surely the envy of all his peers.

'How did you cope with all the competition?' I ask him.

'You mean other available dancers and the wannabes?' he replies. 'There were always younger guys around with more beautiful bodies. It was very precarious.'

I knew about the competition, because I had seen them stacking up in the wings each night. Personally, I could not have borne the continuous threat of someone new. The pressure must have been very tough. But Robert was beautiful and had a body that Rudolf compared to the god Mars, from the Baroque painting by Carlo Saraceni. He was tall, handsome, with curly hair, a strong wide chest, that lovely smile, dignity and that indefinable quality, breeding. As Robert was to tell me, Rudolf liked him because he was an academic, not just a stud.

Three days after their first real meeting, Robert moved in to Rudolf's hotel in New York. There, Robert learned Rudolf's routine of massages, baths, breakfast.

The mornings were spent watching *I Love Lucy*, the 1950s American sitcom with Lucille Ball, before going to class. Sometimes there were three episodes of the show to watch in a row, and they loved it because, Robert said, 'it was so anarchic'.

Life is very strange. Here I am talking to Rudolf Nureyev's lover and partner, and their routine turns out to be so far removed from my knowledge and assumptions of this icon. I do not know what I expected, but *I Love Lucy* was not on my list. Dance and more dance, of course, but watching sitcoms on television was surprising.

Robert goes on to tell me about Rudolf's belief in the healing power of laughter. He believed in this so much that he sent videotapes of *I Love Lucy* to his friend Margot Fonteyn when she was dying of ovarian cancer. I found this incredibly moving. I had read that Rudolf had paid a lot of her hospital bills but this final touch was a very personal gesture. It seemed to say, 'I enjoy this and I know you will too, and I am sure it will help you.' A visual message that said, 'I cannot actually be with you, so here is what I watch, I hope it helps.'

What was it like waking up in bed beside him each morning,

when Robert first met him, how did he gauge what mood Rudolf was in before the schedule of warm-up and classes and rehearsals began?

'That was always tricky. I would always get up early, pack my bag, eat and get his stuff ready, depending on what time he was having a massage. Later in the relationship, I never knew if he had a good night's sleep or not, but I would know right away if it was going to be a crazy day. If he was in a bad mood, I would just be really quiet. After we got back together, I had made that conscious decision to be his houseboy, not his stud, and that basically I would follow through with him for the whole of the odyssey, no matter what.

'But later on it was difficult. Rudolf was always comparing me to how he, Rudolf, had behaved with Erik, even after we had been together for years. He would say that "You do not do *such and such* as you used to". But it was ten years later and we had all changed. He would go on and on about how he had done everything for Erik [Bruhn] at the beginning, even shine his shoes. But I did not want to do all this and be the same. We are all different and I definitely was not Erik. But, I did shine his shoes eventually. I even sewed his ballet slippers. I really did not want to do that, as you normally do your own. It can be so dangerous if anything happens.'

There were some intimate memories of things that make lovers laugh. Robert was playing the cook in *Le Bourgeois Gentilhomme* and was always serving champagne to Rudolf on stage when they met. 'I was always carrying the champagne either on stage or in real life. It was always a big joke. We used to laugh about that,' remembers Robert. It is a warm memory.

As I talk with Robert, I try to imagine what it must have been like to have suddenly been enveloped by this huge personality, this star. Aside from the lust and passion of a new love affair, he must have spent time looking at his reflection and asking if it had really happened, the haunting 'Why me?'. And then, later, to have had to deal with the so-called tantrums and impossible behaviour that became part of the Nureyev legend.

There was an edge to some of Robert's remarks as he said that he had been misrepresented in some of the books about Nureyev as someone who was not a dancer at all until he met Rudolf, which 'just was not true'. In fact, he was selected to be one of the few for the great choreographer and artistic director George Balanchine. This was a huge honour and one that was strongly contested.

'That should speak for itself.' If he had not been able to dance, he would not have been chosen. The competition was always intense for roles, as at any audition, but especially for Balanchine.

If Robert had not been beautiful then Rudolf would not have given him a second glance. As it was, Rudolf pursued him. Rudolf believed Robert to be a great dancer. Robert says that Rudolf had told a friend that he 'wanted to hire a theatre and invite all his friends so that they could see Robert jump'. As I listened to people who knew Nureyev, this wish to show off his new-found lover and his skill began to make sense. I heard from so many people about how Rudolf would help any dancer and teach them, almost nurture them. Rudolf would also have been proud that this new lover was a dancer, not just a night-time pick-up or a bit of 'rough trade', but someone with courtesy and brains.

Rudolf wanted to teach Robert the Bluebird role, from *The Sleeping Beauty*, the role in which Rudolf had made his name in the early '60s. But Robert said that he knew his limitations and had other plans. Rudolf understood, as they both had their own lives.

'What were those plans?'

'I wanted to be a dance historian and a writer.' Both of which Robert has achieved.

I ask Robert what was the great mainstay of this long-lasting relationship.

'He gave me great trust and friendship. He did not take my youth; he shared it with me. He was always talking about my youth. He felt his own youth was being taken away from him. At the age of 25, I did not understand. I had no idea I was going to go through it myself. He shared his wisdom, knowledge and experience.

'It was a master–apprentice role as well. One thing that attracted Rudolf to me was that I was an academic not a stud.'

Robert was intelligent and educated, from a solid middle-class background. He was the son of an English teacher in Massachusetts. He had studied Latin and Greek at New York University.

Rudolf learned and absorbed social graces, perhaps savoir-faire, from Robert and Robert in turn learned about art and appreciation of art and antiques from Rudolf, as well as the artistry of dancing and performing. Robert talked of learning by osmosis and also said that, as a dance historian, what could have been better than to have lived with Rudolf for all those years and learned from him.

Robert's knowledge and interests were broad-ranging. I felt humbled by someone whose knowledge was so much greater than mine on this fascinating subject. Many questions are being asked about ballet and the world of dance. Not least, whether ballet is a dying art form. Robert is sure that it is. He feels that there are too few full-length ballets and that ballet seems to have a rather fragile future, even with the emergence of movies like *Billy Elliott* to inspire more people to cultivate an interest in this art.

Robert says that Rudolf 'was more famous than Michael Jackson'. He was a very complicated man who had been forced to go to school in his sisters' clothes, yet by the time I met him spoke five languages. A man who could 'have' anyone he wanted yet paid for sex. He disliked people prying into his life and even Robert was not allowed to ask questions. Rudolf would snap at him, 'Are you trying to interview me?' time after time. I understand this to mean that he was now a star, and, like all celebrities, he just got bored with being asked the same questions over and over again.

I would find it very hard to accept such a response from someone so close to me, and I am sure that Robert found it frustrating even though he accepted it. If you are starting a new relationship with someone, you want to know everything almost instantly so that you can absorb this person into your life.

But dancing was the key to their friendship.

'Rudolf would have gone to watch dance anywhere, wherever he was in the world, and would dance anywhere to bring entertainment and pleasure.'

When I ask what their daily routine had been after *I Love Lucy*, the answer is, of course, dance, dance and more dance.

To maintain their level of fitness and to position themselves within the company, most dancers perform their own stretches and warm-up before the class as well. Warming up for the warm-up. It is an endless unrelenting journey each and every day to keep their bodies ready and in peak condition. Nureyev, I knew, was obsessive about class – in Violette Verdy's description, it was 'one of Rudi's sacred cows'.

Robert remembers how he personally used to go straight to class without a stretching or bending warm-up of his own, until he learned how crucial it was.

A dancer's class is physically gruelling: the body is pushed and tuned to extremes and the focus is intense. As the newest recruit to a company you can find yourself standing beside the world's greatest at the barre in class. You have to remind your body continuously of all the positions. You must warm it up, stretch it and make impossible demands of a body that has probably performed the night before. You must constantly keep looking in the mirror that surrounds you: check the line of your arms, your shoulders, the height of your legs, the angle of your head and neck. You must do this daily, whether for performance or for rehearsals. Then, whether a star or a new member of the company, you must allow whoever is taking class, be they a fellow dancer, the ballet master or mistress or a guest, to correct and advise you, no matter who you are.

Yet in the middle of all this fanatical pursuit of perfection there is that constant but tricky pursuit of the ideal of balance: between career and a love life, between work and play, between growing up and staying young.

I was beginning to get a picture of their day-to-day routine. Robert took me through an exhausting schedule with up to three shows a night, parties and bed at 5 a.m. But their self-discipline and years of routine meant that they would always be in class.

'Robert, where did Rudolf get his ballet shoes from?' I knew he had small feet, just a size seven.

'All over the place, sometimes Freeds, anywhere at the start. Then towards the end he started wearing shoes by Chacott as they were so soft. I wore Chacott because I believed they made my foot a better shape.'

I have heard dancers say that they cannot walk when they first get up in the morning, that it takes a lot of pain just to stand up. 'First thing in the morning, when I got out of bed, after all those hours en pointe, I couldn't put my heels on the ground, I had to wear high heel shoes until long after I had my shower,' remembers Violette Verdy.

Robert is dismissive that Rudolf had this problem. I knew he had a bad back and a painful spur on his foot, but it is Robert now who says he has trouble getting up with his back, not Rudolf then.

I wanted to know how this idyllic relationship had foundered after just one year.

Whilst they were in Caracas, Robert accepted a lift home from a guy whom Rudolf had his eye on for himself. There was a huge row. Robert pointed out that the man was heterosexual and he had just been giving Robert a lift. But this explanation ended with a black eye for Robert after Rudolf punched him. It was the catalyst for their one and only break-up, even though Robert's memories of waking up on the plane the next day with Rudolf stroking his hair meant a lot to him. 'I thought that was beautiful.'

Robert was starting to write and Rudolf had research to do so they went their separate ways for just eight months. 'We had our own lives to lead.' In that case, I wondered, what had prompted Violette to call on Robert to come back to Rudolf?

'Robert was a very good dancer and a wonderful company member and, of course, good to have around for Rudolf. You know Robert was a great leveller for Rudolf and kept him going through the bad times by continuing with the dinner parties so that Rudolf felt that it was still the same, that nothing had changed – his dancing or his popularity. Robert had such great savoir-faire and was a master of diplomacy.' Softly spoken, with a wonderful lilt to her accent, Violette has all the time in the world for Robert and Rudolf.

I know what she means about Robert's diplomacy. Even when he is speaking about people that he knows Rudolf absolutely hated but who thought they were part of the inner sanctum, there is no question of 'allowing' me or anyone else to reveal the truth. It was enough that he knew. And as to why Rudolf endured these people, I think that it was all part of the challenges he liked to throw down, his games, which I learned about later on.

So what happened when they were reunited in 1980, did they just pick up where they had left off? Robert explains that they did not sleep together when they were reunited as Rudolf claimed that 'you could be friends once you had got sex out of the way'. I wondered if he was happy with that decision and his subsequent role in Rudolf's life. Apparently he was. He made a choice to be Rudolf's houseboy, even to clean his shoes. Robert is firm that he was not a victim: this was his choice and he was happy to do it. He refers back to the 'helicopters, Concorde and caviar lifestyle'.

Robert knew he was lucky. 'He was Russian: if he had not liked me, we would not have stayed friends for 14 years.'

I asked Robert about the infamous court case and listened as he explained how he had heard about the money that Rudolf had left him in his will and realised that the sum would not even cover his medical expenses, as Robert was by then HIV positive. He had stayed with Nureyev for the 14 years, through good and bad times, 'for the whole of the odyssey', and felt that he should have more money than was stated in the will. He tried to speak to his friend, but at this time Rudolf was very ill and being protected by the Nureyev Foundation. So Robert ended up taking his friend and ex-lover to court. The settlement that Robert eventually received had a proviso, or as I call it a 'gagging order', which stipulated that he was not to give any interviews or write about his relationship with Rudolf.

I therefore wondered how Robert was now able to speak to me about his life with Rudolf and he explained that the gagging order had lapsed as he was called to give evidence for the Nureyev Foundation in court, when one of Rudolf's sisters was trying to obtain one of his properties.

'I don't know why they are so scared of me, about what I would say,' said Robert. The 'they' refers to the Nureyev Foundation. I know that there are two Nureyev foundations: one a medical foundation to assist dancers and the other the main organisation that protects Nureyev's money, assets and heritage. It was this second foundation that had opposed Robert's claim to his friend's money.

From our conversation I felt that Robert was sad about the whole process and astounded that it was not until years later that he heard that his friend had wanted to settle with him out of court. The settlement that was eventually reached was for annual payments to be made to Robert but it doesn't take much to work out that as the last payment of the settlement to Robert was in 2000, this was presumably meant to be when he was dead. There still seems to be a lot of animosity surrounding Robert and his court case, and the two factions for and against him are still very much present.

We stopped for the night. I was exhausted and Robert sounded tired. It was some ludicrous hour and I was aware that we had opened a lot of memory boxes. We agreed to speak the next day. I was left sitting on the edge of my bed, phone in hand, and in emotional turmoil. I realised how cold I was. This conversation had stirred up a lot of memories for me. Not just about Rudolf, but about the rest of my life at the time: what I was doing and who I was with. When was the last time I had seen Rudolf and what had happened, and then trying to get the years in some sort of sane and sensible order. I am lucky that my father always drilled it into me to 'keep a diary or at least write it down'.

I was too excited to sleep, so I started one of those crazy middle-of-the-night obsessive missions. I just had to find the Zurich Ballet photo that Rudolf had signed for me. I live in a tiny house, what a friend of mine jokingly calls a 'cabin', but you would think that I lived in a mansion the amount of time it took me to go through all the boxes. I was in a complete panic that the very safe place where I thought I had put it would turn out to be a distant mis-memory.

I did find it, carefully preserved in its much-battered, precarious state. Thank heavens. There they all were. Smiling. Zurich Ballet, Rudolf, Yoko and Dame Ninette de Valois. All the sights, sounds and smells of that moment came back to me as if I was, once again, standing downstage watching this fantastic moment. If I turned it just so against the light, then I could just make out Rudi's handwriting – 'To Caroline, with love from Rudolf'. But it is stuck to the glass of the frame and needs some professional tender loving care to preserve it for my lifetime.

Needless to say, I did not sleep much that night.

When I spoke to Robert the next day, he told me of his dream from the night before. It seemed so real and was very beautiful.

They were on Rhodes; Robert was coming down a path towards the beach and saw Rudolf waving to him from the sea. Robert went into the water to join him and they swam off together. Maybe it was prompted by the lovely photo that Robert has of the two of them on the island of Rhodes in 1980. They look so happy.

I could hear Robert smile.

We learned some more about each other at the start of this conversation. We both have elderly parents and laugh about them being '80 years old with attitude'. It was common ground that was not about Rudolf.

I mentioned to Robert that I had recently watched a video that contained scenes from the musical *The King and I,* one of Rudi's later performances. I also told him about an interview in the video with an usherette who had watched a great many performances of this show. On the video, she could only talk about Nureyev warming up and 'using his cell phone all the time he was practising'.

Robert replied 'He used to go mad about his cell phone bill. It was usually $1,000 a month and he accused me of using it all the time, and that was why it was costing him so much. I never touched it, but he was running *Nureyev and Friends*, Paris Opéra Ballet and all his life on this phone wherever he was. He used to go mad at this bill.'

We are all used to a nomadic existence in the theatre and I had once asked Rudolf where he considered home to be.

'Why?'

'I am curious. You spend so much time on the road I thought there must be a place that you look forward to going back to?'

'Here, there, I do not know. It is a theatre where I dance, a hotel where I sleep?' Rudolf shrugged.

It was a well-rehearsed interview response and seemed to fit with Robert's story about being accused of 'interviewing' Rudolf.

So I asked Robert where Rudolf was happiest and he started with the house on St Barts. He hesitated for a moment and searched for the word that Rudolf used to describe it. 'What did he used to call it? – That's it, a "dog house".' This does not translate well into English and so Robert described it for me – a plain four-square wooden house with four bedrooms, a beachside house. It does not sound remotely kennel-like. It was on the 'rough' side of St Barts, near the nudist beach. They were not troubled by photographers, tourists or residents. It does sound idyllic: a house where Rudolf played Bach through the night and videos were watched. This time it was Charlie Chaplin videos.

Robert then recited the list of homes. 'At one point it was ten. The house in Richmond, the flat in Fulham, which is where we would stay in London because it was nearer to the theatres. Then there was the villa in Monte Carlo, a penthouse in Monaco, the islands in Italy, Isole dei Galli, St Barts, Paris and the ranch in Virginia.' Rudolf had apparently wanted to open a dance academy at the ranch. He wanted to turn all the barns into dormitories and have Robert teach dance. I wondered why it had not happened, but it just seems to have been lost as an idea in the '80s.

Robert still sounds slightly amazed that Rudolf once sent him out to buy a beautiful flat in the Dakota Building in New York. Now that is some responsibility, even if you are very close to someone and are very confident that you know their taste and desires. With Rudolf's temperament, it was even more of a challenge and did not turn out to be a great success. Rudolf accused Robert of buying him 'a lot of corridors'. That was the first apartment and then they moved to the second floor with wonderful views over Central Park and Lauren Bacall as a neighbour. Their stories of domesticity include mundane anecdotes of overflowing washing machines and apologising to neighbours.

What about the places in London?

Robert said, 'It was mad buying a house in Richmond. The traffic always made us late.' There doesn't seem to be much logic as to which place they stayed at in London and why.

The descriptions of Rudolf's homes are fantastic. Large, opulent, sumptuous and filled with valuable works of art and antiques. 'The walls were covered with paintings of male nudes,' Robert recalled. I thought that all these homes must have been quite dark. Robert said that as 'Rudolf was out of the nineteenth-century "sensibility", it fitted with the buildings, a love of the nineteenth-century décor.'

Rudolf adored art, architecture and antiques. He had absorbed his love of art from his mentor Nigel Gosling, the former art critic of the *Daily Telegraph*, and passed on this passion to Robert. Rudolf adored Nigel and whenever they were all in London they stayed with or visited Nigel and his wife Maude, even though Rudolf had his own homes in the city.

Robert talks of shopping for antiques no matter where they were. My touring shopping consisted of no more than cheap clothes from wonderful long-gone markets; Rudolf bought Robert a pair of 'knickers', plus-fours, a jumper and socks from Yves St Laurent as a Christmas present. He still has these he laughs, but has never worn them. Then there was the fur hat that Robert is sad that he gave to a girlfriend. It was a present from Rudolf.

Once again we are both tired and we agree to finish for the moment. We make some great plans for me to go and see Robert in New York as soon as I can.

I have always believed in some kind of driven reason for the timing of things. Serendipity or fate had made sure that I had not found Robert when he had had a car crash in the late '90s. He was badly injured and even if I had found him, I wouldn't have been able to speak to him. I was really not meant to find him at that time. Then I realised that I was not meant to start this project until I had also found Bill Akers and Roger Myers.

The stories that Bill and Roger were about to tell were, in true theatrical tradition, going to 'make 'em laugh, make 'em cry'.

CHAPTER TWO

The Haircut

There were two photos in the envelope from Australia. The first was a rather faded colour photo of a beautiful young Nureyev. He is wearing a dark-navy velvet tunic top, trimmed with gold. His hair is swept back and very short. It is a lovely photo. One hand on his hip, he looks as though he is challenging someone.

The second was a huge black-and-white photo with Rudi sitting astride a chair, wearing a towelling dressing gown, with a young man standing beside him, looking as though he is asking Rudi a question.

Scrawled across the bottom of this oversized photo is a dedication from Rudolf to Roger. On a small piece of paper is a note that tells me that the foot I can see in the bottom right-hand corner of the photo belongs to Robert Helpmann, who was playing Don Quixote at that time.

While Robert Tracy was able to give me an insight into what everyday life was like for the older Nureyev, I wondered what he had been like at the beginning, as the young Nureyev, the exotic defector.

I had been talking with a friend of mine, Pamela Foulkes, at the Sydney Opera House, and she had told me about her experiences of working with Rudolf at Australian Ballet in 1973.

At the end of the conversation, I asked her if she knew of anyone else who had known Rudi. Perhaps they did not come from what I called the dinner-party set or the social glitterati, but maybe there could be a worker, someone who, like me, had watched, listened and got to know Rudolf over the years. Or maybe, as I was to discover in this instance, it might be that previous biographers had tried to interview them but they cared so much about Rudolf that they were wary of anything they said ending up in a lurid tale.

This question to Pamela led me to William (Bill) Akers AM (Australia Medal for services to the theatre) and his friend Roger Myers. They were long-standing members of Australian Ballet, in Bill's case of some 38 years. Bill was originally the stage director. He also loved lighting the ballets. He was a long-term friend of Margot Fonteyn, having first met her in 1957. Roger was originally a dancer and had then moved into management.

Bill and Roger wanted to tell their stories, as, 'This is going to be the book that I would never write,' said Bill. 'There is a fear as well, of ending up in your dotage muttering about the famous people you have known and some nurse telling you, "There, there, you will feel better after your medication"!' They had not spoken to other biographers, they told me, as, 'it seemed that everyone was out to denigrate Rudolf, and even when it was not meant to be fantasy it might as well have been'.

When Rudolf came to Australia to perform with the Ballet in 1964, Roger was a dancer who later became his personal assistant. Roger and Bill's relationship with Rudi was to last until his death, nearly 30 years. The last time that Bill saw him was three weeks before he died.

After our first telephone conversation, which ran us through laughter, memories and tears, they said they would put it all on tape. I spent a week anxiously waiting for the first of these. These were stories that they had told each other and to friends for years. I do not think that it was that easy for them, though, as they stirred up a lot of memories. They were late-night recordings made, Bill said, 'when the mood was with me'. The tapes were wonderful.

I had asked Bill to tell me on the tapes anything that occurred to him, but to start at the beginning and explain how their 30-year friendship had come about.

'Everywhere you turned in 1962 was the name Rudi. His name was literally everywhere. I came across him for the first time in a letter sent by one of my team from Paris. He had watched Rudi's performance with the Marquis de Cuevas Ballet. What struck me most from this letter was not the talk of people throwing underpants and stuff onto the stage but the throwing of coins. Rudi had just kept on dancing, even though coins were landing everywhere. He was totally focused on what he was doing and that is how I remember him when he was dancing. Focused, giving us everything.

'One day, I walked into the theatre where we were working with Australian Ballet and someone said to me in an excited whisper "Rudi's here".

'I said, "Who's Rudi? Oh, you mean Nureyev." I had not met him before and I did not know that he was coming to see us, let alone that he was dancing at this precise moment on the stage. He was not performing with us, so I was curious. It was 1962, and I learned that he had flown from London to see Erik Bruhn perform. I went down to the stage and then saw this extraordinary creature warming up in the middle of the stage.

'I realised that this was Nureyev.

'The stage can be a tricky place. Whilst it looks like a nice, clear, open box, anything could be happening that you do not automatically see. He was very young and extremely beautiful, but I remembered that he was suing someone for an injury that had occurred on the stage somewhere and I did not want us to be put in that position so I asked him to leave the stage. I reminded him that we were starting with *Rendezvous* that night and that there was no overture, so there was really very little time left for him to get off the stage. He obviously knew the piece and was leaving it until the very last moment to stop dancing. He glared at me and stormed off to Erik Bruhn's dressing-room. I adored Erik, he was an absolute prince, and I still think that he was the greatest classical dancer ever.

'Well, Rudolf did not look that happy and, of course, during the show, there was a complaint that I had asked him to leave. I reminded the manager about the legal problems and he agreed that I had done the right thing.

'Halfway through *Rendezvous*, Sonia Arova [with whom Bruhn had had an affair when he was 18] came down to the stage to find me. She said that Nureyev had an injury and would I go and look at it. She was pleading with me as she said it was "a bit tense".

'I went into Erik Bruhn's dressing-room and there was Nureyev, this beautiful young man, lying on a chaise-longue. He was clutching his calf. Erik said that he had a problem with his leg. Everyone knew I had a background in physio, which is why they had asked me to come down to see him. I always looked after Margot on tour as well.

'I felt his leg and then felt the other one. Nureyev just lay there. I turned to Erik, as I did not know if Nureyev even spoke English at that stage, and said, "Erik, unless your friend gets urgent attention on his legs, he will not be able to dance any more."

'From behind me came this amazing voice. "I am very aware of it. I have to earn a lot of money very quickly."

'I replied to Rudolf, "Unless you do seek help, you will not be making money dancing at all soon."

'"Who are you?" he demanded in that wonderful accent.

'"It doesn't matter who I am, you must get some treatment and very quickly." Which he did. He knew he had to. He went to the States and got treatment, retrained and when I next saw him on a late-night TV show from the States, he was dancing a pas de deux and looked tremendous.

'Then the next time I saw Rudolf was later, in 1964. His picture was all over the Australian press. It was the usual build-up to his arrival, the pre-publicity. There he was doing his huit entrechats or dix entrechats; he used to do so many. He had this mop of blond hair. His hair was quite long and in this picture his hair was flying out and looked like an umbrella. Besides which it looked sissy, and that was not the Australian image, nor the one for the ballet company. So, I spoke to James Levine, the manager, and said that Rudolf needed to get a haircut. You can imagine that there was quite a bit of, "You tell him", "No, you tell him", going on between the pair of us. This was not going to be an easy task but James said that he would tell him and that I would have to arrange for the barber. I wanted to say "Why me?" but I did it. I booked Rudolf an appointment with Angelo de Marco.

'When he came into the theatre with his new haircut he just glared at me. I was stunned; he looked absolutely sensational.

'"You look wonderful," I said.

'He glared at me, flared his nostrils and said, "You have made me look like a lesbian." So, I thought, that is good, we seem to be getting on then!'

Listening and speaking to Bill and Roger was a fantastic opportunity to hear about the young Rudolf. They had worked with him, talked to him and gone out 'hunting' with him during the glory days of his career.

I recounted to Bill Rudi's remark to Robert whenever Robert asked him a question: 'Are you trying to interview me?'

Bill said, 'It was easy to ask him questions in the beginning. He was happy to talk. Don't forget he was a very young man in his 20s when I first met him and I was in my mid-30s. I suppose it was his thirst for knowledge and he hadn't got bored with being asked questions about his life, his past, at this stage.

'We were sitting in the stalls one day during a lighting session and I had always wanted to know how he got that scar on his lip.'

– Now, I had never asked Rudi about this and would never have dreamed of doing so. That mouth was so extraordinary and sensuous. The scar made it even more unusual; it became an extraordinary mouth. The scar added to the whole image, the exoticness of Nureyev. –

'So, one day I just asked him, "How did you get that scar?" and Rudi replied that a dog had bitten him. I asked, without thinking at all, if it had been a Great Dane. Well, I really had not intended this to be the joke it turned out to be and I was horrified. I realised what I had said and that he would think that I had meant Erik Bruhn, as the "Great Dane". But Rudi thought this was hysterically funny. He was roaring with laughter and sat there with tears of laughter running down his face. The more I said "No, I really did mean what sort of dog, Rudi, honestly", the more it made him laugh.'

Bill roars with laughter at this memory.

'You know, his dancing was extraordinary,' said Bill, 'when he was doing something controlled or contained like Albrecht in *Giselle,* he was wonderful. But, sometimes, when he let it go, for example in *Corsaire*, it was almost too much to watch, it was so breathtaking. You could tell how much he was enjoying himself. His costume was tiny; there was really nothing of it at all. You could hear the audience gasp as he started the famous solo.

'He came off into the prompt corner and asked me, "What do you think, baby?"

'"You're killing 'em, kid, get back on!" Well, he was a young man and enjoying himself.'

I asked Bill and Roger about some of the day-to-day routine that they both went through with Rudi. I wondered if the young Rudolf did anything differently to the older Rudolf.

Roger explained, 'Everyday it was the same thing: tea and toast and *Gilligan's Island* on television. I spent my life making tea for him. The programme started at about five thirty every evening and we had to be at class for six. But Rudi would watch all of it, which only left us five minutes to get to the theatre. I used to say to him, "We must go now, Rudi", but he would watch it right up until the very last moment, even the credits. We would then pile into my tiny car and head out into the rush hour. He would be screaming at me, "Faster, Roger, faster, Roger", but we were stuck in rush hour. Every night it was the same thing. We would get to the theatre so late that he would have to do a private barre at the back of the stage and then join in, every single night.'

Bill added, 'Rudi was mad about *Sesame Street* as well, but he drove us all crazy by calling it "Se Same Street".' He was incredibly good at making jokes with words, playing around with the meaning and sound.

What about his thirst for knowledge, what Robert called his 'learning by osmosis'?

Most of the people that I spoke to were struck by his voracity for learning and this 'engine' that drove him almost manically. Bill told me that, 'He always said to me that he knew he was not going to live long, it was as if he knew something was going to happen to him.

'He was very different. You see most dancers do not develop their minds or their brains. It is not that they aren't able to; it is just that they are born to dance, so their bodies are their main focus. Rudolf was different and he knew it. He was aware that this was almost his destiny and he needed to learn everything and do everything so very quickly. It was incredible to watch.'

Roger Myers remembers, 'He read all the time. Everywhere you looked, he was always reading something. I once spent hours looking for a book for him.

'He really liked Virginia Woolf and he was very keen to find a book of hers. I decided, as this seemed to be so important to him, that I would go and try to find him a copy. We were on tour at the time in the States. None of the bookshops had any Virginia Woolf at all so I ended up at Harvard in the campus bookshop and luckily I found him a copy. I cannot remember which one it was now, but he was incredibly grateful. "Roger, you do everything for me."'

I asked Bill about the more mundane parts of their lives.

'You know, Rudi was very careful about what he had to eat. So was Margot,' said Bill. 'They were very aware that if anything made them ill and we had to put on understudies then it would not go down well with the audience, who had basically come to see the pair of them. It was more than the problem of letting anyone down or the trouble it would cause. They were acutely aware of the amount of money it would cost in ticket refunds.

'When we were in New York, we went to the Russian Tea Rooms with him and he always had the same: scrambled eggs then steak, with vodka to drink.'

Robert had clear memories of the Russian Tea Rooms. 'The first time we went there I ordered a tuna sandwich and Rudolf was furious. "How can you be so American?" he was screaming at me. "Why didn't you order caviar?" Robert laughs at the memory. He said I was "so American" when really I was just a student on a student grant. I always had a tuna sandwich.'

Even at mealtimes, his temper or temperament shone through, as Bill explains. 'Meals out with him could be a performance all by themselves, Roger and I always had to remember whose turn it was to go and hide in the loo when we went out to eat with Rudi. He always had the same thing after a show: an enormous T-bone steak. He liked this to almost still be walking. The steak was not the problem, though; it was the smoked salmon he always ordered before the steak. He would throw this at the poor waiter screaming, "It is too salty. In Russia it is not salty."

'We used to get through the meal somehow, then on this one occasion Roger and I were taking him back to the hotel, the Windsor hotel in Adelaide. As I held the door open to Roger's car, he kissed me on both cheeks and said to me, "We must not fight so much. You are so temperamental; you always have to have the last word." Well I could have killed him, he was describing himself not me.'

I had been to parties and meals with him on various occasions where the drink was liberally supplied. Robert told me, 'Oh, sure, drink was not a problem.' Some of the books I had read seemed to imply that he was an alcoholic, but I had never seen him drink or be drunk during a performance. Perhaps his drinking to excess was a response to a gruelling day, or, as a friend of mine commented, that as a Russian 'everything was done to excess!'

I wondered if some of the challenges that we had all been set were just part of his humour. I asked Bill Akers.

'Whenever he took a curtain call at the beginning in the '60s, which was that amazing bow, then the right arm up to the gods and down again, he never ever smiled. I said to him one night after a call, "Please will you smile, just for once?"

'He replied, "Not until they are ripping up the seats."

'Well, the calls were a show in themselves. Solos from either side from Margot and then Rudolf, then together again – they lasted sometimes as long as the ballets themselves.

'Rudolf went out for his next solo and the side of his mouth just twitched a little. Then, when he went on the next time as he finished his bow he smiled broadly at everyone. It made front-page headlines in the papers the next day, "Nureyev smiles". Just imagine what it must have been like to make the front pages of all the newspapers and all because you smiled.'

Roger Myers went to collect him from the airport in the early '60s and as they drove through town, Rudolf saw huge posters of his face on the side of all the trams pronouncing that 'Nureyev is coming'. 'Rudolf found this hysterical and when he finished laughing he just looked at me and said, "Yes, but when?" That was his sense of humour.'

I heard a lovely story about Rudi's first taste of English 'farce' and humour. It was the swinging '60s and British tastes were in a state of flux. Like the rest of the world, we had just been introduced to the lavish, glamorous lifestyle of a spy named James Bond. Given a chance, we would all pile into our local cinemas to watch the obvious and gloriously outrageous *Carry On* movies. Our taste at the theatre also leaned towards the ludicrous. A knee-jerk reaction, perhaps, to so many years of austerity.

Farce became the thing to watch and we revelled in it. Semi-clad girls ran round the stage whilst a myriad of doors, with perfect timing, opened and closed to men predisposed to lose their trousers. They were very much of the time and far removed from our politically correct twenty-first century. Rudolf landed in England right in the middle of this.

Adam Harrison, a stage manager who worked with me one year for the Nureyev Festival, suggested that I contact Brian Rix, now Lord Rix, as he remembered a story about Nureyev going backstage at one of these farces. I was surprised, as it sounded highly unlikely. The story, though, became even more improbable when Lord Rix spoke to me.

Lord Rix, associated with British farce for years, tells this tale of how a mediocre production called *Who's Your Father?* became the fantastically successful *Chase Me Comrade*, and of the two stars who came to see it.

'Ray Cooney had written a new farce *Who's Your Father?* It was about an escaped convict. It opened in Richmond, on the outskirts of London, but it really wasn't very funny.

'Now, Ray swears that this is true. He was driving through Trafalgar Square and saw Rudolf Nureyev and decided to rewrite the play. He wanted to call it *Chase Me Comrade* and base it on a defecting Russian ballet dancer. We opened it at Windsor and it really was very funny. Kerry Gardner played the Nureyev character. He had to learn Russian and be taught a Cossack dance for the show, but he really did look like Nureyev.

'The play transferred to the Whitehall Theatre in 1964, in August. A few weeks after it had opened, Margot Fonteyn came to see the show.

'The next time she came she had Nureyev with her. She had told him that he "had to see it". A farce is a very visual show, so, although his English may have been minimal, he would have understood the comedy.

'I thought that Margot Fonteyn was a wonderful person and I was thrilled when she and Nureyev came backstage afterwards to my dressing-room. We had a few large Scotches and we were having a great time. I have no idea what Nureyev thought of what happened next.

'An old friend of mine, who was appearing in the show, had a rather disconcerting party trick. Forget the *Puppetry Of The Penis* show from a couple of years ago. This man had been doing it all that time ago in the '60s. It helped that he was very well endowed and could do bizarre things with his penis. He suddenly joined us in my dressing-room and began to go through his routine. But as he was performing for my VIP guests, Margot Fonteyn and Rudolf Nureyev, all of us with a few drinks inside us, all I could think was that the man from the *Daily Express* newspaper's William Hickey page was still in the theatre. I dare not think what would have happened if he had found out what Fonteyn and Nureyev had been offered as post-performance entertainment that night. Doesn't bear thinking about!

'The strange thing was that when we had a cast change, the new guy who was going to play the Nureyev character was a real Russian who had lived in Australia with his family; he had trained as a dancer and obviously spoke Russian.'

Bill Akers loved Rudi's sense of humour and recalled: 'Rudi was standing on the edge of the stage in San Francisco by the prompt corner, warming up, doing his baton frappé. He said to me, "Bill", or "Beel" as it sounded, "Have you seen my lover?" I laughed and said, "Which one?"

'"Do not be so cheeky, I mean Mr Wallace."

'"Who?"

'"Mr Wallace Potts."

'I was laughing with him and saying, "What sort of a name is that for heaven's sake. Have you brought him over from England?"

'"He is very tall. Very beautiful. He is from Texas. You will find him leaning against something."

'I said that I would go and look for this Mr Wallace Potts. I walked around the theatre and when I got to the back of the opera house, there were windows out onto the street and there he was.

'I could see this beautiful, tall young man, wearing the most expensive suit, and sure enough he was leaning against the building. I signalled him to go to the stage door and met him there. He was about 6 ft 2 or 3 in. tall.

'I took him down to the prompt corner and left him in front of

Rudi. Well, Rudi did not take any notice of him for a long while. I was fascinated. Then he said, "Wallace, suit is very beautiful." He had had it made for him in Paris by Yves St Laurent. I then took Wallace to Rudi's dressing-room.

'For the whole of this tour the crew had been complaining about a huge, very heavy box that we had to carry everywhere for Rudi. It was about 6 ft long and really heavy. It went into Rudi's dressing-room at each theatre. We had no idea what was in it.

'I left Wallace in Rudi's dressing-room and said that Rudi was warming up and would come to the dressing-room soon. Wallace said that he knew all about that, so I left him and went back onto the stage. Rudi asked me, "Has he got his weights?" Of course, that was what was in this wretched box! No wonder we had all had such a hard time lugging it around all the theatres. And, sure enough, there was Wallace changed out of that wonderful suit doing his weight training in Rudi's dressing-room. Rudi said jokingly, "I like to keep my men fit."'

I told Bill about my own personal challenges set by Nureyev and that I knew how difficult it was to be accepted by him. I explained that it took me three years to gain entry to his private world or even the space surrounding him. I had watched as naive young dancers tried to attract Rudolf's attention by performing right in front of him, speaking to him through their bodies in dance. They were unaware of all the hurdles you had to surmount to be allowed in. They were usually stopped from doing this by ballet mistresses under the pretext that they would annoy Rudolf while he was practising, though more realistically they were worried that the youngsters could turn better or faster than he could by then. But I do not think he was interested. Amused, certainly, but as he had not called the shots, and he had not ordered them to do anything, it seemed to be irrelevant to him.

But Rudolf had good reason to be wary of those around him, as the threat of the KGB still haunted him, even many years after his defection.

There is a particular story of Rudolf's trip to Australia to see Erik Bruhn in 1962. The plane was refuelling in Cairo and he had persuaded the flight attendants to let him stay on board. He apparently saw some men walking towards the plane in unnecessarily heavy winter overcoats for Cairo. Instinctively, he knew they were KGB looking for him and hid in the lavatory. The stewardess protected him by showing the men an empty plane. This incident, happening so soon after his defection, must have been a terrifying experience and the memory of it would have been particularly difficult to shake off.

'In the 1965–6 tour with Australian Ballet, we flew to Los Angeles,' remembers Bill Akers. 'We were playing the Dorothy Chandler Pavilion, which is really a wonderful theatre. When we arrived, there were security guards everywhere, or rather the Hollywood version. Rudolf panicked. Really panicked. He felt very threatened and it took hours to convince him that they were there to protect him, not harm him. He really believed they were there to arrest him. We eventually coaxed him out of his dressing-room by assuring him that the guards would stand out of his view on the edges of the stage. But he was really upset by that experience. We had the same problem in Berlin, where he probably had more reason to fear that the KGB would grab him at any moment to take him back to Russia.'

I had no understanding of what this spectre of the KGB must have been like until I worked on a ballet gala at Drury Lane.

The Bolshoi star Maris Liepa was dancing. There is little or no time for rehearsal at galas like these. People are giving their time usually for free and fitting it into impossible schedules. They fly in, perform and then fly out again. All I needed to know from this lovely smiling guy was when he wanted the curtain to go up: on an empty stage, or revealing him already there. We mimed these questions beautifully between the two of us in sign language and laughs, with a few 'tah-dah's thrown in for good measure. As I approached to confirm with him my understanding of our comical mime, two bouncers – crew-cut hair, pale-grey shiny suits – appeared from nowhere to halt my progress. I realised that this was the KGB, stopping my subtle communication or anything else. We were held apart at arm's length just by their presence as we attempted to conduct what was a professional conversation. I could see the mute acceptance but frustration in Liepa's eyes at this intervention. I suppose that we owed some of this to Rudolf and his 'escape'.

The crew at the Coliseum had told me that they had KGB with them on the fly floor during the visit of the Bolshoi in the early '70s. They had spent every performance watching over the edge of the fly floor, looking at all the dancers. It was a very clever place to watch as you could see everything: a great vantage point. They watched them constantly while they were on stage and I do not think they were mad-keen ballet fans.

No wonder Rudolf watched everyone around him and trusted no one until he was absolutely sure of their intentions.

It also explained that 'look'. Not the flare of Tartar nostrils but the slightly hooded gaze of someone watching from the centre of the stage, looking into the gloom of the wings and scrutinising the unknown people watching him. The same look I used to get whilst sitting in the wings, miles away. I would know that I was being watched; I could feel it. Rudi would always catch me talking to one of the crew when we had just laughed about something. I would glance up to see 'that look'.

My partner at the time was watching from the wings one night when I looked up to see him scurrying away to the stage manager's office. He found the way Rudolf was staring at him 'unnerving', and as he could not interpret it, he decided to retreat. 'I did not know what he wanted.'

We were at Régines nightclub in London one night. The whole company was there, promoters, sponsors, theatre management, everyone. It was a beautiful evening, a hot summer's night, and the roof garden restaurant had been reserved for us.

That night at Régines, I remember turning around to have a good stare to see who I could spot. There, in the centre of the room, was Rudolf. He was sitting slightly back from his table, wearing his omnipresent hat and an oversized multicoloured jacket. He looked detached, slightly irritated and he was watching. He was looking at everyone, assessing them and waiting for the minutes to go by until he could escape into the night to go to another party or to go hunting. To the uninitiated, his bearing would have appeared imperious, arrogant and grand. He was the very epitome of the star at the number-one table.

Rudolf was the only person I have ever known who, when you

caught his eye, gave no smile or nod of recognition, just a continuation of the look. It was the ultimate 'Who do you think you're looking at?' He was like this with everyone. And sometimes this was just an indication of what was to follow.

Violette Verdy remembers, 'He used to study people, question them and you could see him slowly assessing whether they were going to be worth it, worth knowing. He watched to see what he was going to learn or get from them. He used to say of people that you had to get to the bottom of it, what they wanted. Then they passed and survived.

'Once you had passed all Rudi's tests as a friend then he would be loyal to you for life. He would always be there for you. But if anyone let him down then his treatment of that person could be almost fatal. He was like a modern Genghis Khan.'

He also did not allow friendship to prevent him from exhibiting his fearsome temper.

'You hate me don't you?' asked Rudolf.

'Yes.' replied Bill Akers.

'Pig, *pisstushka*.'

'He could be impossible. I used to put on Rudi's body make-up for *Hamlet*. *Hamlet* is incredibly difficult whether you are an actor, singer or dancer. He had to look very pale and Danish. Well, we weren't having such a good time as I was putting this stuff on him, and he knew what I thought about him.

'One year we were in Paris at the Théâtre des Champs-Elysées and the evening turned into a bit of a farce. I went up the stairs to use the toilet and as I slammed the door shut – I know that this sounds like too much information, but stay with me – the bolt shot out from the other side and I was locked in. This particular toilet had a French window that I could open and I remember standing on it and waving to the secretary in the window opposite. Obviously she could not hear me, but she looked up at my frantic sign language for, "Help! I'm trapped and there's a press call in a few minutes and I am meant to be down there helping Rudi." She probably looked at this and thought, "Oh, God, another mad Australian", and she then totally ignored me.

'I was now in a panic, what a stupid thing to have happened, and

I had no idea how I was going to get out of there. Thankfully, we had been given little gifts on our arrival, small badges, things like that, and I had been given a letter opener, a souvenir of Paris, which I had put in my pocket. So, just as I was really about to worry, I managed to slip the hook back on the lock with the letter opener and make my escape.

'By this time I could hear all this pandemonium on the stairs outside, screaming and shouting. I had no idea what was happening.

'I opened the door just as Peggy van Praagh, one of the co-directors of Australian Ballet, ran past me saying that Rudi had thrown a wastepaper basket at her. When I arrived at his dressing-room, Margot was just leaving and there was a guy on the floor with a bruise on his face.

'I discovered that Rudi had been put into some trousers for a photo shoot. He had bent over to do his make-up and they split from front to back. He was furious, and as he wore absolutely nothing underneath costumes, he went like that to our wardrobe mistress Frances. He stood there naked, waving the trousers in the air at her, and said, "Fix them." Frances was horrified at this apparition standing in front of her, and said to Rudi, "I only fix ladies' clothes."

'He was furious, incandescent, at this.

'Rudi headed back for his dressing-room and began to trash it, he threw a wastepaper basket out of the door just as Peggy van Praagh was passing. Then this poor man got in the way so Rudi punched him and then left, disappearing down the Champs-Elysées wearing only a raincoat.

'In the midst of all this, Margot had come along the corridor to see what the trouble was and had made a hasty retreat. So we had a trashed dressing-room, a guy with a bashed-up face and a half-naked Nureyev running round Paris. What a drama.

'One day we were rehearsing for a RAD gala and he was in a terrible mood. He just sat on the edge of the stage and wouldn't move. It was only when I threatened to replace him with Garth, one of our dancers, that he moved. I have no idea what was wrong with him.

'I never confronted him about these scenes and the next day when you came in, everything was back to normal. I just dealt with it on a professional level and said, "It is a new day let's get on with it." To have delved into it at the time would have made it all so much worse.'

I told Bill about how shy I thought Nureyev was, and how he used his body to express himself rather than vocalise things, even to the extent of just walking away if he didn't want to discuss something further. This was easier for him. But his temper was sometimes incredibly irrational and I asked Bill what he thought was the root of it.

'I still believe that his temper stemmed from his frustration that he wanted to be perfect, but his body was not and in his opinion it could not ever be.

'When we were in Liverpool, I had been to see the movie of *The Sleeping Beauty,* the ballet, of course. Yuri Soloviev was dancing but with horrendous make-up that made him look like Betty Boo. He had huge red lips with lipstick. I told Rudi all about this, but also about how wonderfully he had danced.

'"Ah, yes," said Rudi, "we were at school together. The difficulty we both have is that our thighs are too short. Top of thigh to knee too short."'

Bill explained: 'Which meant that neither of them looked like "premiers danseurs nobles", while, of course, Erik Bruhn did. It was all to do with proportion and line, which was crucial for a true "prince", a classical ballet dancer. It must have been a continuous niggle at the very least for him, watching himself whilst practising and comparing himself to others, knowing or believing that he was not perfect.

'When he came back to us in Australia in 1964, he was beginning to get a reputation for being difficult. But over the years of watching him and seeing how much he cared, how much ballet meant to him, I began to understand. He wanted perfection, but he knew that his body couldn't deliver perfection, so that's why he got so frustrated.'

I understood now why he had always altered his costumes. There is a famous story about *Marguerite and Armand,* created for Fonteyn and Nureyev, when Nureyev shortened the tails on his jacket much to the dismay of all as they felt it made him look ridiculous. By making the jacket or tunic so much shorter, however, he gained a few illusory inches to his leg length, and, of course, he showed off his body more. It had seemed like pure vanity until you realised he was creating a diversion from his thigh length. It is interesting that such a beautiful creature should still have a vulnerability or paranoia about himself.

I wondered if Bill Akers had ever seen Rudolf argue with Margot Fonteyn.

'Rudolf would do whatever Margot said. Even right at the start when I first worked with both of them, Rudolf would always acquiesce to her.

'I think that *Giselle*, and specifically Act 2, is probably the best ballet in the repertoire. I loved lighting it and one day Rudi and Margot came onto the stage to see what had been done. Rudi looked at it and called to me in the stalls, "Honey darling." Honey darling? I turned to Peggy van Praagh and said to her, "Does he mean me?" Well, I stood up and went down to the stage and he said to me, "Honey darling, atmosphere is beautiful, very beautiful. I do not think we need follow spots."

'Margot immediately said, "Rudi, people are paying an enormous amount to see us" – it was six guineas, which was a lot then – "and they should be able to see us for that amount of money." Rudi immediately said, "Yes, Margot," with no question. He was always learning from her, you see.'

Pamela Foulkes was able to add more about his temper and tests. 'I joined Australian Ballet in 1973. It was my very first theatre job and I was overawed,' she told me. 'I had never been abroad before but found myself in Moscow and then travelling all over Europe. It was a wonderful time. Then we came to London with *Don Quixote*, and on top of all that we were performing at the London Coliseum with Rudolf Nureyev.

'He was really awful to me. I was the lowest of the low in the company at first, just an assistant stage manager. You know the tables and chairs in the inn in *Don Quixote*? Well, every night I would check that they were on their "marks" and exactly where they should be, and every night he used to come down to the prompt corner and hiss at me, "Move the fucking tables, they are too far upstage."

'Now, Rudi's whisper could be heard at the back of the circle. It was not subtle. Every night I put them on their marks and every night he would edge them downstage, screaming at me each time that the "fucking tables" were too far upstage.

'One night I had had enough, first job or not I just cracked and shouted back at him, "If you move the fucking tables any further downstage, then they will be in the fucking orchestra pit." He just glared at me, but I had done something right as I kept putting the tables in their correct marked positions and each night as he passed the prompt corner I waited for the usual tirade, but now all I got was an eye sparkle. He positively twinkled at me.'

I wondered just how many hours a day Rudolf had spent working out tests such as the tables for Pamela, the nakedness for me and all the little challenges that we had to take on before we were accepted.

I had witnessed the verbal displays of his temper but never the physical ones. They were over as quickly as they started. Robert was the one who had to work out which mood he was going to be in every day. I just turned up at the theatre and felt the atmosphere on the stage, around his dressing-room and looked at the dynamics of the other dancers. I did not have to work out what breakfast was going to be like. 'We were both Pisceans,' Robert said, 'so we understood each other.'

I had, however, witnessed what Rudi and Robert called his 'self - explosions'. It would be easy to say 'who hadn't?' They were infamous, widely reported in newspapers and carried with them rumours of ashtrays being thrown, vacuum flasks and coffee cups flung at people and even whole rehearsal barres. Robert says that he has these outbursts of temper, too.

These self-explosions were huge, immediate, vast eruptions that stunned everyone within earshot or throwing distance as target practice.

But if you use your body to express yourself and have done for nearly all your life, either in dance or any other physical activity, then mustn't it be nearly impossible to tell someone what the problem is? Wouldn't Rudolf have automatically used his body rather than some strange device like speech, even though he became fluent in five languages?

I asked Robert if it was true, the story of Rudolf at Franco Zeffirelli's villa the night that he had reportedly defecated on the steps, having supposedly been locked out. I suppose I was hoping that it was fiction. Sadly, I had met too many people who knew someone who had 'been there'.

Robert said Rudolf's outrageous act was done not because he had been locked out or had been later than anyone else. As Robert said, Rudi could have just rung the bell to be let in.

Robert explained: 'Zeffirelli did not cast him in *La Traviata* and Rudolf was furious. Zeffirelli chose Vasiliev over Rudolf.' Of course, Rudolf's career was waning and to add insult to injury he had been at school with Vladimir Vasiliev. 'Rudolf then trashed Zeffirelli's villa. They made it up afterwards, though.'

'Do you remember Rudi's nightly routine?' I asked Robert. 'The enormous rows about the announcements I was always threatening to make and how he was always stark naked when we had our "contretemps"?' Robert laughed and said that a lot of people would envy me.

I never worked it out, whether Rudi did this just to shock me, or maybe he was just late. For years when I was working with him, I thought he used our nightly 'discussions' as a way to fire himself up with adrenalin ready for the show. I was happiest with that answer.

Pamela Foulkes remembered another of his 'games'.

'One night it was a wonderful balmy autumn evening, and we had all been sitting on the wall opposite the stage door in Bedfordbury waiting for Rudi to arrive. I had just decided to move over the street to the stage door when Rudi roared round the corner, being driven by some guy. He mounted the pavement to park and just kept driving at me. I suppose I had a moment of "Aussie stubbornness" and I refused to move. The car had to screech to a halt but it only just missed me. As Rudolf got out, he twinkled at me.'

One night, however, I was forced into a confrontation with Rudi after the show. Instead of the normal drawn-out sequence of curtain calls, Rudolf did just a few and then exited the stage. As a result, we were left with an audience baying for their idol. Certainly, leave them wanting more, but this was hopeless.

I had no idea what had happened and I was really cross. It went totally against the grain: 2,232 people had paid to see their hero and wanted to show their appreciation but it seemed that he couldn't be bothered. I went to his dressing-room. He was surrounded by visitors but I still went in, fired up by adrenalin and obviously with something of a death wish.

'What on earth is the matter?' I demanded. 'If there was a problem, tell me! Don't just walk off like that!' I was scaring myself. 'It is hopeless to do that to your audience.' Adrenalin is a dangerous thing.

I remember that the guests were stunned. So was I. I hadn't done this for years: confronted someone with their lack of professionalism. One of the guests turned – to admonish me I assumed – but Rudolf just waved his hand at them. As I felt that I was not going to get an explanation, and indeed realised I should not be speaking to him about it in front of his visitors, I put it down to experience, said 'Good night, see you tomorrow' and left quickly.

I wondered what the mob at the stage door would be like having been robbed of their full 30 minutes of adulation and put my head down and grunted a reply when the stage doorkeepers asked if Rudi was on his way. There were hundreds of people waiting as usual. I had a feeling that they would get short shrift that night.

Rudolf's love of confrontation and gamesmanship did not stop at anyone. One night he wanted to see Robert and a woman have a row in a restaurant. He stage managed it and then sat back as tales of foul language came back to entertain him.

Roger Myers remembers, 'He hated flying, and when one of the stewards came round to check that he had fastened his seatbelt, Rudolf punched him. It was awful.'

My conversations with Bill and Roger in Australia always took place on Saturdays. It suited me: I could call them at 8 a.m. UK time and speak to them before they settled in for their evening.

Roger told me about their routine on Saturdays in Australia. 'We are allowed to spend Saturday lunchtimes reminiscing. It is an important part of our week. It keeps everyone's memories alive. We sit around having lunch and saying, "Do you remember so and so and when such and such happened?" We are allowed to cry on Saturdays.'

Roger recalled, 'Because I was working as Rudi's PA, I had got to know him very well. There was the endless tea and toast routine – "more tea Roger", nearly 24 hours a day.

'One time we were having an accommodation crisis. I had to move Rudolf from Bobby Helpmann's apartment because he didn't like it. I had to call in favours from friends everywhere to sort this out. It is difficult to describe the apartment. It was in an old building and was at the top, probably best described as like maid's quarters. There was nothing really wrong with it other than it wasn't what Rudolf expected. So I contacted various friends and moved him out to a local hotel, and then ferried him from theatre to hotel and back again in my small car.

'We were still going through the nightly routine of watching *Gilligan's Island* each and every evening, and being late. Apart from the tea and toast, I had the onerous task of washing out his jockstraps as well.'

Roger laughs at this thought, while Bill comments wryly, 'Lucky Roger!'

Roger also had some very serious and difficult tasks.

'In 1970, one day we got the most dreadful news at Australian Ballet. Alexander Pushkin, Rudi's teacher, friend, father-figure, mentor, from the Kirov, had died. Pushkin had been crucial to Rudolf during his training at the Kirov. Rudolf used to stay with Pushkin and his wife, and you know how his wife seduced Rudolf before his first exam performance. They must have been like a family to him.

'There was a lot of controversy about the circumstances surrounding his death. Whether he had been left to die out in the snow, what had really happened, so many stories, and there had been rumours of rows at the Kirov. It was awful.

'Well, because I was Rudi's assistant, I was asked to go and break the news to him. I was terrified because I knew how hard this would hit him. I knew how much Pushkin meant to him, just as we all did. This was someone still in Russia. He was part of Rudi's life and more than that, of course, part of the life in Russia that he had left behind. This man was very much part of his career and his very existence. I had only had to tell someone once before that someone else had died. It is a dreadful thing to have to do.

'I decided that the only way that I could do it was to go straight in to see him and come straight out with it.

'"Rudi, I have some awful news. Pushkin is dead."

'"What? When? Where was he?"

'"They found him lying in the snow."

I wanted to know so much more about this, where they were, what happened the rest of the day. How did the rest of the company react to this sad news? Did Rudi speak to Roger about this later on? But I realised that Roger was crying at the memory and I just could not ask any more.

'Well, he started to cry. He crumpled, and the only thing I could do was to just take him in my arms and comfort him.

'I just held him in my arms and he cried.'

CHAPTER THREE

The Nureyev Dress

'To Rudolf.'

Robert and I clinked ice-cold glasses of champagne together.

'We should be drinking Bellinis. That was Rudolf's favourite drink,' Robert said as our glasses touched.

'I don't think my jet lag could cope with peaches and champagne!'

But champagne had been Robert's choice.

Robert and I met for the first time in 18 years in June 2003. We were in New York and I felt as if I was on a roller-coaster high of adrenalin, nervous anticipation and pure child-like excitement. Of course, I had been up since 3 a.m., out of sync with everything and wondering what this meeting would hold. I hate jet lag. I was ready to organise the world, but maybe not at 3 a.m. I had so much to ask Robert face-to-face and I couldn't wait to see him again.

I had set Robert what I realised in retrospect was a near-impossible task, as it would be in London or any city with so many styles, choices and areas to choose from: 'Why don't you choose somewhere for lunch?'

For Robert, however, the choice had been easy.

'Cipriani's at Grand Central Station. Cipriani's in Venice [Harry's Bar] was Rudolf's favourite restaurant in the whole world.'

I had not been to Venice for years and I had never been to Cipriani's. I knew the New York Cipriani's was in a station, but to call Grand Central just a station is like calling Hampton Court Palace just another palace or the Taj Mahal just another tomb.

I arrived a good 20 minutes early and walked down one of the bright tunnels into the huge central hall. I was stunned by the opulence and splendour of the place and stood gazing at all the marble, taking in the details until I saw on the first level the Italianate arched sign for 'Cipriani's Dolce'.

I chose a table in the corner and sat down to wait and look out over the travellers as they crossed from one side of the station to the other. Somehow, in that extraordinary space, even the names of the various lines and their destinations as they clacked up on the timetables created a sense of adventure and allure.

I had a lot to ask Robert. I wanted to hear about the women in Rudolf's life and, of course, about his relationship with Margot Fonteyn. How much of what had been written about them was speculation and how much did Robert know?

I spotted Robert coming from one of the side entrances and I am sure we both made a determined effort to pretend not to have seen one another. It would have spoiled the impact of actually meeting and greeting one another after all these years.

Then, there he was, standing by the table. Tall, with the hair that I remembered. He was thinner and now wore serious black-rimmed glasses, but he was still the same Robert.

It was so easy. We smiled, greeted and embraced one another, and picked up exactly where we had left off. I congratulated him on his choice of restaurant and we then proceeded to keep all the waiters at bay for hours as we talked and talked.

I had brought him two presents, both of which I really hoped would not only be surprises but also hold special meaning for him.

My father, an old Fleet Street journalist for some 52 years, had worked for the *Daily Mirror*. The paper had a tradition of presenting leather-bound albums to the Royal Household after any state occasion. They were embossed with the newspaper's name and the details of the event. I had found a lot of letters in my father's desk from the Royal Household, thanking him for these.

One such letter stood out, as it was from someone totally different but highly significant to me. It was from Margot Fonteyn. It was flimsy, delicate, slightly yellowing and the handwriting had faded, but her name was printed clearly on the top of the cream paper. My father explained that she was the only person outside the Royal Family for whom the newspaper had prepared an album. This precious letter thanked my father for the selection of photos that he had sent her following her honeymoon with Tito de Arias. She requested some more and asked if she could be a 'nuisance' as she wanted to keep some of them as well. As she also had the album, I think that these extra photos were for her personal use. It was a charming letter and very special.

I had come across the second present or surprise by chance while rummaging through a cardboard box in a shop in Gees Court, one of the lovely Georgian-style narrow pedestrian passages linking St Martin's Lane to Charing Cross Road. This is a wonderful part of London and I can lose myself for hours looking through its bookshops, art shops and theatrical memorabilia collections. In one of these treasure troves, hidden amongst hundreds of Royal Opera House and London Coliseum programmes, was a beautiful bright-red programme from the Royal Opera House dated 1964. It was for *Swan Lake* with Rudolf Nureyev and Margot Fonteyn. As I bought it, the proprietor said rather fiercely, 'You've got a bargain there.' It must have been lying in the shop for years. I thought I had got a bargain, too, and something quite precious. To watch Robert open it and go straight for the picture of Rudolf was wonderful.

'Ah! Here is Rudolf looking beautiful.' I was embarrassed in a way, as it was such a small gift, but Robert disagreed, saying it was 'before his time' and that this was the sort of thing that he was missing. 'The Rudolf before I knew him.'

I noticed a man at one of the other tables watching this small presentation ceremony with amusement. We must have looked like five year olds disguised as forty-somethings.

We talked and talked and tried to order food. We both finally decided and our waiter, who was a very easy-on-the-eye young guy, succumbed to Robert's quizzing: the sort that is actually badly disguised pure full-on flirting. In the conversation that ensued, we learned that he was Egyptian and was looking forward to seeing his girlfriend. He had not seen her for two years. This prompted Robert to tell him that we had not seen each other for 18 years and the waiter looked stunned. Robert said, 'We have taken up exactly where we left off.'

I jokingly suggested to Robert that he should come back here to see the waiter again. Robert laughed and told me about a party that Rudolf and he attended in St Moritz, where both of them were looking at the waiters.

Rudolf had said to Robert, 'We should be in the kitchens with the waiters. We would have more fun.'

I remarked to Robert about how beautiful Grand Central Station was and he told me that it was Jackie Onassis, then Kennedy, who had campaigned in the '60s to prevent it from being demolished. This was the same Jackie O who had campaigned to get Rudi's mother out of Russia and also for Rudolf to get a visa in order to see her. When he finally did get to return to see his mother in 1987, he made Jackie promise that she would rescue him if anyone attempted to prevent him leaving Russia again. She promised him that she would, but it turned out not to be necessary.

Jackie first met Rudolf when he was dancing with Margot in New York in the 1960s and she sent a plane to bring them to the White House to meet them for tea. She remained friends with Robert and Rudolf right up until the end and was one of the few people whom Robert informed that Rudolf actually had Aids.

Robert tells of happy holidays with Jackie in Greece and of being photographed by paparazzi. Jackie was sunbathing naked but, with such a beautiful body, she looked wonderful.

I asked Robert when we had first been talking whom he had meant when he said that Rudolf had slept with three women. I had read about various women in his life who were implicated, but I wondered what Robert thought. I teased him by asking if Jackie O was one of them. Robert was horrified 'Jackie! What? No. She disliked sex.' I thought of all the images I had seen of Jackie Onassis in which she looked so perfect, beautifully coiffured and always in haute couture, and recalled a great quote from her about sex: 'Sex is a bad thing because it rumples the clothes.' Maybe that was all it meant to her.

There are stories that she did not actually sleep with Aristotle Onassis before they got married and now I can see how this might have continued even after they were married. Onassis stayed on board his yacht, the *Christina*, which Jackie found vulgar, while

Jackie stayed in their home. They were eating separately and living separately.

Jackie was said to have been horrified by the tall bar stools in the bar on the *Christina*, which were covered in whale scrotum. Onassis used to enjoy asking each woman who sat on the stools, 'What is it like to sit on the largest balls in the world?' He would not change them even for Jackie. They sounded grotesque. In that setting, Jackie must have felt very alone. I began to see what she had meant when she said about marriage: 'The first time is for love, the second for money and the third for companionship'.

I also started to understand why Rudolf and she got on so well. If she was not interested in sex, then out of all the women who pursued him she was one of the few who met him on equal ground, wanting no more than friendship. Like Rudi, she was world famous. She knew what the pressures of celebrity meant. She had also been through some terrible times and perhaps that was another link to Rudolf. That, like him, Jackie had been through so much to get where she was.

I had read that Jackie Onassis was the only woman that Rudolf would stand up for in his dressing-room. I never met her but this reminded me that whenever I went in to see him or was summoned, he would be sitting putting on or taking off his make-up, whilst whoever was there stood beside him. But obviously Jackie Onassis was different. I had also seen a letter from Jackie to Margot Fonteyn where she says that she is 'no longer going to call Rudolf "Mister Nureyev", having spent the whole evening dancing on his toes'.

Later, it was to Rudolf's ranch in Virginia that Jackie went to visit whilst riding her horses. She enjoyed the parties there whilst friends were flown in from New York and Rudolf played Bach on the huge organ that took up a whole room.

It must have been refreshing for Rudolf and there must have been a lot of trust between them. Robert has a lovely photo taken in 1992 in New York with Rudolf, Jackie and himself. One of the last happy memories of the three of them.

These memories of Jackie Onassis started us on the fascinating topic of the women in Rudolf's life. Robert had told me when we were speaking about Rudolf, their break-up and the women in their lives, that they were both bisexual and this was when he had made the comment that there were three women with whom Rudolf had had sex.

I had read that Rudolf had slept with Xenia Jurgensen, the wife of Pushkin, his ballet master at the Kirov. Robert agreed that she was one of them. Presumably one of the others was Maria Tallchief, one of the four wives of George Balanchine, an ex-prima ballerina with New York City Ballet and Ballet Russe de Monte Carlo. She had also had a relationship with Erik Bruhn and, as mentioned earlier, it was Maria who introduced Rudi to Erik.

So that was two of the three. I had to ask about Margot Fonteyn.

She was a British icon. The prima ballerina assoluta and a household name. She was so very much loved by the public. The relationship between Rudolf and Margot appeared wonderfully ambiguous. You could make up your own story to fit your personal dream about these two wonderful dancers. We knew that this ballerina in her 40s had re-ignited her career thanks to a Russian exile in his 20s, and we wondered if she had possibly also found something more.

Every photo and story of them was eagerly devoured, including those of their arrest in the US at a party where marijuana was being smoked. To watch them perform *Romeo and Juliet* was to see a performance so compelling that it was difficult to believe that their passion did not continue off stage.

Robert was adamant that I would not make him 'say it' – that Margot and Rudolf had been lovers. It leaves a lot of room for speculation, particularly as others have claimed that the stories were true. I can understand his reluctance to discuss their relationship, however, as it falls in with my belief that there should always be some areas of a person's life that are private.

I prefer to leave it to the imagination, the wonderful photos of the two of them and, of course, the film of them dancing together. But the ending to their story is not that wonderful.

In May 1990, Rudolf danced at a fundraising gala in honour of Margot, who was by then terribly ill, as was Rudolf. He was so angry at his performance that he would not stay afterwards. He stormed off and out of the theatre and was quoted as saying that she, Margot, 'did not need him any more', although he was finally persuaded to return for the celebrations. This was a complete contrast to earlier that day when he had carried her down the stairs as she was not able to walk down them by herself. Margot Fonteyn died on 21 February 1991. She had not known that Rudolf was ill. Nureyev couldn't bear to go to her funeral. Instead he hid and mourned her in private on St Barts.

I knew how much she meant to him. He had displayed it so clearly to me one night at the Coliseum. I had received a message from the stage door, the phone ringing loudly on the prompt corner and everyone turning round to stare at me accusingly. A basket of flowers had arrived for Dame Margot Fonteyn.

The basket arrived and it was enormous, in fact almost vulgar, ribbons dangled from the handles and around the front of a huge basket of roses. It stood about 5 ft high and it was not an easy object to miss. It had obviously been chosen with care and probably in the hope that we would present it on stage.

It stood in solitary splendour in the wings whilst I thought about this problem; dancers occasionally stopped to read the card and excitedly told each other who it was for. We were mid-performance of *Don Quixote*.

Well, I knew that she wasn't dancing that night and that this delivery would be a challenge. Perhaps she was in the audience?

During one of Rudi's exits I asked him if he was expecting Margot. In a classic example of miscommunication, he thought I had said that she was in and his face looked astounded. 'Margot, here tonight?' He was overjoyed.

'No, wait,' too late. I didn't have time to explain as he went on again. The whole of his next solo was probably danced for her.

I remember thinking, 'Oh God, how did that happen?' And so, I and various camera-hunting ushers and people in the box office spent a fruitless half-hour discovering that she was not, after all, in the house.

On his next exit, he rushed up to me, 'Did you find her?'

'No, I am sorry, we didn't. I think it must be a mistake.'

Rudi looked devastated, crestfallen.

I knew that there was a lot still to learn about Rudi and Margot's relationship, and as Bill Akers had told me that he had known her since 1957, I was sure that he would be able to shed some light on this fairy-tale relationship. So I left the subject of Margot for a later time.

But now I wanted to ask how a Russian child who played in the streets and sold pencils in the mud related to royalty, a royalty that was mostly female. Socialising with members of the highest echelons of society was an integral part of Rudolf's life at that time. Robert described meeting Princess Michael of Kent, Princess Sarah of Jordan and Diana, Princess of Wales. He singled out Princess Michael of Kent as a particular favourite of his and Rudolf's and told me that there had been a beautiful photo of the three of them together. Rudolf had said that it could not be used, however, because Robert was in it. I was amazed at this but he just shrugged and told me: 'Well, we had our own thing. We did not go around publicising anything. Once we were interviewed and I was described as his "assistant".'

Robert also remembered meeting Princess Diana and how much both he and Rudolf liked her. But they did not have the opportunity to meet her that often or get to know her very well. He then went on to cite a list of British, European and Middle Eastern royalty, and a roll-call of famous surnames from wealthy families that seemed endless. I noticed, however, that one royal person was missing from Robert's line-up.

Princess Margaret was integral to ballet in the UK, and she featured throughout my career as a stage manager, as did so many other members of the Royal Family. She became the patron of everything balletic and a constant ballet-goer. There were photos of Nureyev and Fonteyn with HRH all through the '60s and '70s.

I was, therefore, intrigued by Robert's response when I asked him to tell me about his meetings with Princess Margaret. He replied briefly, 'Sorry, she was before my time.'

'But it was 1979 and you were with Rudolf until 1993, where was she for almost 14 years?' I asked.

'Sorry, I cannot help you, I never met her.'

Royal galas are a part of the life of any theatre, perhaps more so with ballet and opera. You get used to the routines and foibles, the security before each performance and the line-ups of the stars ready to meet the royal guests after the show.

I used to have a rough time with Princess Margaret. I do not expect that I was alone in this. She was at every single gala bar one that I worked on. Protocol requires that the audience must be in and seated, and therefore the cast ready on stage or backstage, prior to the arrival of any member of the Royal Family. This leads to a Catch-22 situation: if you get the cast down too soon and the audience is not back, then everyone niggles. Equally, you cannot have the royal party returning to the royal box when no one is ready for them.

Princess Margaret and I seemed to have a game going at every gala. We started smoothly and the first interval went well, but the rot would set in at the second interval when the front-of-house manager would come back saying that HRH was getting irritated with the way I was hurrying her. I was not aware that I had been hurrying her, as I had been ringing the bar bells as usual.

Of course at the next interval I delayed the bells to the last possible moment to allow her time to finish her drink and this time I was caught out by her returning early. There was no audience in, no orchestra in the pit and no cast on stage. I had been well and truly beaten at this game. It was incredibly frustrating.

Then, in 1989, at a private visit to Earls Court to watch *Carmen*, she was a totally different person. I found myself 'volunteered' to escort her round and introduce her to all the principals. Funny how everyone else had something very important to do, and it was stupid really as she would have been much happier and it would have been more appropriate had she been escorted by a man. The Chinese mezzo-soprano Ning Liang was singing the role of Carmen that night. It was right after the Tiananmen Square massacre. Horrific reports were coming in and Ning was worried for her family. When I mentioned this to Princess Margaret as a prompt for something to talk about whilst meeting the cast, she went straight over to Ning to talk to her. When she came back, HRH asked me to repeat her name for her and said quietly, 'Tell her later that I will say a prayer for her parents tonight.' She meant it.

But what happened to Princess Margaret, the most famous of English ballet fans? Robert obviously did not know. As a child during the '60s I have memories not only of Rudolf's defection but photo after photo of Princess Margaret in fabulous puffball cocktail dresses and evening gowns meeting ballet stars. There are reports of her accompanying Lord Snowdon whilst he took photos of Rudolf and Margot at rehearsals and got the all-elusive scoop for the newspapers. All the other papers had to wait until the more public rehearsals, but they had been pipped to the post by Lord Snowdon. The royal couple apparently had great fun with Margot and Rudolf, laughing and joking.

A quote from *The Times* emphasises the enjoyment that Princess Margaret had at these meetings, describing how her face lit up with 'a smile of unfeigned delight and genuine engagement' when she met Rudolf and Margot in a line-up after a performance. There are also vivid descriptions of Rudolf turning up to one of Princess Margaret's parties during the 1970s as part of 'the Margaret set'. 'He was dressed flamboyantly either head to toe in tight-fitting leather or in a full-length fur coat.'

The Princess laughed off newspaper stories that Rudolf was giving her ballet lessons, saying she found them 'hysterical' and that they were just close friends. Her description of Rudolf in a newspaper interview is an insight into the impact he made on her: 'Here was this creature from the moon. He was more beautiful than I can describe with his flared nostrils, huge eyes and high cheekbones . . . a new species of animal.'

Pamela Foulkes remembers a fabulous party on stage at the London Coliseum after a performance of *Don Quixote*. Pamela and I first met at the English National Opera during the '70s. Tall, slim, blonde and quietly spoken, Pamela was another people-watcher but with intellectual astuteness and a great Aussie-style cynicism about everything the world threw at her. Pamela was just 23 at this point and it was the first time she had worked with Rudolf.

'It was a wonderful party after the show and it was held on the stage, which was unusual. Everyone who was anyone was there: film stars, VIPs and Princess Margaret and Lord Snowdon. Princess Margaret came to see Rudi all the time.

'I remember making a lunge for the last bottle of champagne and finding myself in an arm-wrestling contest with Lord Snowdon for this last bottle!

'I drifted towards a group of people which included Princess Margaret and Peggy van Praagh. We were standing upstage by some of the tables used in the ballet.

'With a completely straight face, the Princess said that it was such a shame that her sister the Queen had not been there to see the wonderful horse.

'Now, this was a pantomime horse and just used by the dancers. We had no idea how to respond as she had such a straight face – was she joking or serious? I had to run behind a piece of scenery, it was hysterical.' Pamela laughs at this memory.

But back in New York, Robert Tracy was adamant that this particular ballet fan was not known to him. 'You are intrigued, aren't you?' he said.

'Yes, Robert, I am. What on earth happened to her over those years?'

'I don't know, I really didn't meet her.'

In 1978, a year after she attended the premiere of *Valentino*, Princess Margaret had her own journey to make. She was divorcing Lord Snowdon and was bearing the brunt of attacks by MPs about her workload versus the money she received from the Civil List. Roddy Llewellyn, her 'beau', was about to have orders from 'on high' to leave the country for a few months and *The Sun* newspaper ran a headline 'Give Up Roddy or Quit'. It was not the happiest of times. On a tour to Australia, she caught pneumonia.

The Royal Family was reported to be opposed to her relationship with Roddy Llewellyn and his 'hippy set'. Perhaps they associated Nureyev with this group and felt that her associations were getting her such a bad press that she should distance herself from this flamboyant Russian. I do not know. The last record of her attending a performance in which Nureyev appeared at the Royal Opera House was in 1977, for *The Sleeping Beauty*.

She certainly did not lose her love of ballet, as she was there for Margot at her benefit gala in 1990 when Rudolf danced. But, during the intervening years from 1977 to 1990, they appear not to have seen one another. There appeared to be no record at the Royal Opera House or the London Coliseum of any gala or performance by Nureyev that Princess Margaret attended.

I became more and more intrigued when researching this. There are so few references to Nureyev in the biographies of Princess Margaret, in fact just one sentence in one. In one book on Nureyev there are no references at all to Princess Margaret.

Perhaps her social engagements and royal duties just prevented her from attending his performances for 14 years, but I do not believe that for one moment. I could understand that she may have been instructed not to associate with Nureyev any more but still cannot believe that with her personality she would have just caved in and agreed. I began to wonder if she had felt with Rudolf and Margot that two was company and three was a crowd, but why she should do this after all these years I do not know. Maybe she tried a little too hard to get to know Rudolf and he rebuffed her? That, to me, seems more likely.

A friend of mine, who was at the Royal Academy of Dramatic Art in the early '50s, says that Princess Margaret was seen as 'possessive' by most of the students. She visited RADA a lot during this time and whenever she was to visit, the best-looking actor was chosen as her escort. This is hardly surprising, but then the women were also all told to stay well away from her during the visit.

I heard another intriguing story about Princess Margaret from a journalist, who told me that a British rock and pop star found himself the focus of Princess Margaret's attentions. He was appearing in a musical in London's West End in the '80s, when he received a summons from the Princess. Apparently she had been to see this musical night after night and was madly in love with him. A limo was sent for him and he was taken to Kensington Palace. He was wearing just jeans and a T-shirt and felt rather underdressed for such a summons.

On his arrival he was shown into a large room where there were already quite a few men, drinking champagne while sitting on chairs in rows.

Princess Margaret herself then appeared and drew back the curtains dividing the room to reveal some completely naked men being photographed. Embarrassed, and definitely feeling that he was in the wrong place at the wrong time, this particular star made his excuses and left.

It is a bizarre story, but a great shame that he left before seeing all the action.

Perhaps, after her divorce from Lord Snowdon, 'the Margaret set', dissolved. It seems unlikely. There must have been some wonderful parties on Mustique. There are reports of her staying there with lots of young men, but no Nureyev. When I spoke to Roddy Llewellyn, he said that he had only met Nureyev once, in 1976. So I was no further on.

Robert and Rudolf met many of the other royals together, but by the time Robert arrived on the scene in 1979, Princess Margaret was not around.

I was frustrated that I could not conclude this intrigue, if indeed there was one at all. Perhaps I would have to settle for 'busy for 14 years'.

I wondered about the women closer to home and specifically the Nureyev family women.

With any relationship you inherit a family. Sooner or later, even if you are not introduced to the parents, you certainly meet all the others and Rudolf's family was no exception. With his father dead and his mother ill back home in Russia, his sisters and niece were about to come into Robert's life. There was not to be much love lost between them.

It came as a shock to Robert to find himself affianced to Rudolf's niece Gouzel, courtesy of Rudolf. In order to get Gouzel out of Russia, whilst President Carter and Jackie Onassis were trying to help Rudolf get back in to Russia to see his mother by petitioning the Russian Government, Rudolf suggested that Robert should marry his niece.

Gouzel sounded quite a character. Robert recalled, 'She looked a lot like Rudolf and she was a dancer, but she was not highly rated and was a real ball-breaker.' I asked Robert if he would have gone ahead with it. 'Of course,' he replied. 'To get her out of Russia.' He was saved from this marriage when Gouzel turned up in New York to stay with Rudolf with her husband whom she had met in South America. It was a lucky escape. All of them living together in the same apartment in New York does not sound that wonderful, as there were frequent rows and bad atmospheres.

'Gouzel was always trying to seduce me because I was Rudolf's boyfriend. She saw me as a challenge.'

Later, whilst Robert was busy writing his book on Martha Graham, he moved into Rudolf's villa outside Monte Carlo to stay and write. However, the protector of this property was Rudolf's sister Rosa.

When Robert arrived at the villa on a warm sultry Mediterranean evening, the gates were firmly shut. All the lights were out and there was no reply to Robert's persistent calling and ringing of the bell, even though Rosa knew that Robert was on his way.

After scaling the walls and the gates, Robert climbed through an open bathroom window, as he knew the house well. Once inside, he met an impassive Rosa walking around the house in total darkness. Robert asked her why she had not let him into his partner's house. Rosa claimed that she had not recognised him when he was ringing and calling – presumably she had been watching – even though they had spoken the day before.

This tale becomes more Hitchcock-like in its telling. Rosa spent each and every night awake, walking around, checking the whole place because she was convinced that the KGB were watching and listening to everything. She even climbed up ladders to look at the telephone wires. Robert kept well out of her way, working and writing in the daytime and avoiding Rosa on her night-time prowls. They barely communicated with each other. Neither of them really understood the other.

Robert also described how Rosa would carry a bucket down the hillside for miles, 'just to get water, and because it was free she would spend all day doing that and the hills were so big, it was just mad, there was water at the villa, of course'. Robert stayed there for a month. I don't think that there was much contact after this between Robert and the Nureyev family, except of course when he was called to give evidence in court.

Robert and I turned for a moment to the subject of children and the 'what if' scenario. Rudolf had started filming *Exposed* in 1981 with Nastassja Kinski as his co-star. She was incredibly beautiful and had captured everyone's imagination in *Tess*. There were reports that she found Rudolf really attractive but that he said firmly that it was 'no', but whether this was an automatic reaction or whether it was a response to an advance by either of them is unclear. With her wide sensuous mouth and broad features, she resembled Rudolf. Robert told me that when she had her baby, a little boy, Rudolf said that that child should have been his but that he could never get rid of her 'minder' for long enough. He also told Robert, 'I would have had two children but both the women had abortions.'

I am quite a possessive person. It is getting better as I am getting older, but I am not good at sharing time or space with anyone if I am in a relationship. I have known both men and women who live in a constant state of tension when anyone comes near their partner or territory and I could sympathise with Robert's tales of the many women in Rudolf's life, to whom he was either romantically attached or who were just 'in the way'. One of those who often 'got in the way' was Douce François, a continual presence in their lives who brings to mind Princess Diana's remark that there 'were three in the marriage'.

Douce François was a ballet-loving heiress, originally from Chile. Her step-uncle was a noted homosexual. I remembered what Violette had told me about this friend of Rudolf's: 'Douce was wonderful, she did everything for Rudolf. You know, she was one of those androgynous women who exist from time to time. She was always beautifully dressed, so elegant; she gave up all her time for Rudolf. She desperately wanted Rudolf's baby.'

'Douce was everywhere,' said Robert. He was quite firm and said that there was definitely something between Rudolf and Douce. Wherever they were in the world then Douce would be there organising or phoning. 'Sometimes I would just find her late at night massaging Rudolf's feet.' But even Douce fell foul of Rudolf's rages and once had a vacuum flask of coffee thrown at her in Paris. After a full-blown row between her and Rudolf, a friend allegedly suggested that she dress up as a man to win her way back into Rudolf's good books.

She must have dreamed that she could change Rudolf. She even had her hair cut to resemble a boy to try and turn him. Perhaps she was searching for a father-figure in Rudolf, to replace her step-uncle, and was therefore prepared to take everything he threw at her. The only way Rudolf could tell her to stop was to use actions not words.

Some previously published biographies quote from his contemporaries at the Kirov and they shed some light on how he treated Douce and most women. He was 'completely indifferent to the female sex' and 'he got on badly with women because he never paid them enough attention'. But if you had been surrounded by them all the time since you were a child then it is understandable that you would try to escape anything that smacked of smothering. As I had learned, if you did not stand up to him right from the start, you were lost. The game was over and he would have no time or patience for you. He would just walk all over you or, worse, ignore you. Douce seemed to have borne the brunt of this behaviour and tolerated it.

There are cruel tales of Rudolf deliberately inviting other women rather than Douce to his homes to make her jealous. Rudolf was using her like a toy, an amusement. But she chased Rudolf and 'nannied' him beyond belief. I read that she took this to such extremes that she 'almost followed Rudolf into the bathroom', and it does seem as though she really was a masochist. Douce, like any of the thousands of women in the audiences around the world, seemed to think that 'if only he had met me first, then it would have been different'. John Lanchbery, the conductor, is quoted as saying that Rudolf used Douce as an 'unpaid secretary'. Of course, but she would not have minded.

And yet Rudolf stood up for Jackie Onassis every time she came into his dressing-room. I wondered what test she had passed and when she had stood up to Rudi in order to gain so much respect.

Our meal drew to a close, and Robert and I prepared to venture out into New York. We said goodbye to each other but you could tell that we were both in a world full of Nureyev after our conversations about his anger, women and life.

I thought about all the women in Rudolf's life and about Robert's remarks. I remembered all the thousands of women who waited after each performance around the world to catch a glimpse of their idol. And working with Rudolf, I saw night after night why he used to wail, 'always the women never the men', as he was interviewed yet again by another female journalist or signed all those autograph books for adoring female fans.

I was reminded of an instance, some years ago, as I was standing in the front-of-house of a provincial British theatre when I saw a well-known actor of stage and screen deliberately hanging around the front of the theatre. He was looking at the star photos and waiting for people to recognise him. He did this every day. Sad? Maybe, but probably part of his addiction to attention and need for reassurance. For a performer, adulation must come at a price. But the attention can be addictive and surely it is flattering even when annoying?

Rudolf was surrounded by beautiful women and men, royalty, socialites and people who told him he was wonderful every step of the way, even the women looking at him with large doe eyes. And maybe on the dull dog days it gave Rudolf something to rant about.

Yet it was all the women who had been his friends that saw him through to the end, bearing the brunt of looking after him when he was ill. Of course, apart from Robert and a few other exceptions, most of the men were dead.

Back in London I remembered Robert's remark about the photograph with Robert, Rudi and Princess Michael of Kent. It prompted me to contact Princess Michael and I was delighted when she agreed to see me.

I got into a black cab at Liverpool Street Station in London, and said to the driver, 'Kensington Palace, please.' He roared with laughter when he heard me and said, 'Well, lady, you've impressed me!'

I had impressed myself.

My driver was one of the old school of talkers, thinkers and philosophers. There ensued 40 minutes of laughter that only ended as we pulled up to the gates and a policeman approached to tell us, 'You can't stop there'. We had parked where the sign had told us to and with incredible patience the driver pointed to the sign beside his cab that instructed taxi drivers to 'stop here'.

I left this debate and seemed to ruin another policeman's day when I told him, 'No, I do not know how to find the private apartments.' He wearily led the way as my escort and guide.

We walked past long, grey, covered walkways bordering tantalising, inviting courtyards. Huge glass lanterns hung down embossed with a gold crown and EIIR. We walked past another open courtyard, this one with beautiful blossom trees. Colourful flower boxes were lined along walls to break up the steel-grey stone of the palace and were offset wonderfully by the black gloss paint on everything around them. It was very pretty.

The tall policeman executed a very well-rehearsed duck under one of the arches, which made me smile. He said that he had learned quickly after knocking his head more than once – even with a helmet, it hurt. He told me about the rows of scratches on the ceilings in St James's Palace, long parallel lines. I had no idea what these could have been until he explained that they were the points of halberds that had scratched their presence hundreds of years ago as the ceilings were so low. Along the way, in the black painted doorways and gates there were other signs of life. Cat flaps and dog flaps gave a sense of friendly domesticity to this royal backstage.

I was led into a very pretty room, with plenty to occupy nervous guests in the way of paintings and prints. With apologies for keeping me waiting and with real warmth, the Princess did not disappoint me.

It is quite an art to be able to go back into another world, in this case some 24 years earlier, no matter how busy you are. The Princess recounted a beautiful story of Rudolf dancing for her and her guests. It was London and 1976. Most of us remember it as the year of the heatwave. The temperatures soared, London parks and commons were watched for peat fires and we all sweltered.

'This was before we were married, when I had my own house,' she told me. Prince Michael had learned to speak Russian and the Princess suggested that he should keep up this newly acquired skill. So she had the idea to invite Rudolf to dinner at her home in Chelsea.

The Princess did not know Rudolf other than from the various occasions that they had met after ballets in the presentation line-ups. But she invited him and was pleased that he accepted.

They were dining outside and there were about ten guests, including Rudolf. It was a steamy, close city evening. Her Royal Highness remembers the moment when Rudolf, wearing a white open-necked shirt stood up and gave an impromptu dance. As she

Bill took this photo of Rudi in 1964, just after he had fallen flat on his behind.
(© William Akers)

Rudolf Nureyev, Dame Ninette de Valois, Yoko Morishita and the directors and dancers of Zurich Ballet on stage at the London Coliseum in 1980.
(© From the author's collection, photographer unknown)

Rudolf and Robert on holiday in Rhodes, Greece, in 1980.
(© Robert Tracy)

Robert Tracy in New York in 2002.
(© From the author's collection)

Violette Verdy – seen here teaching students at the University of Indiana.
(© University of Indiana)

Rudolf in Australia as Actaeon in 1964. (© W.F. Stringer collection, Rudolf Nureyev in *Diana and Actaeon*, the Australian Ballet, 1964. National Library of Australia. Photo no: 6558/148)

'Roger was always making him tea, and Rudi had a soft spot for Roger.' Rudolf and Roger Myers during a rehearsal of *Don Quixote* in Australia. (© William Akers and Roger Myers)

Jackie Onassis, Rudolf and Robert in New York in 1991.
(© Robert Tracy, photographer unknown)

Princess Margaret, Dame Margot Fonteyn and Rudolf Nureyev at the premiere of *Valentino* in 1977.
(© Press Association)

Rudolf rehearsing in street clothes with Yoko Morishita
on stage in Manchester, 20 June 1983.
(© *Manchester Evening News*)

Yoko warming up oblivious to the stage crew in London in 1985. 'The stage-left wings were very small.' (© Carolyn Soutar)

Rudi and Yoko with the corps de ballet of the Matsuyama Ballet, Tokyo (Swan Lake) in London in 1985. (© Carolyn Soutar)

In the late '80s, when Rudi returned to Manchester,
it was obvious that the years had taken their toll.
(© *Manchester Evening News*)

told me this story, I could see that she was back there watching and what an impression this moment out of time had made on her and her guests. Prince Michael of Kent also got the opportunity to practise his Russian with Rudolf. This story explained the intriguing pile of Russian magazines left for visitors to read while waiting for their appointment with the Princess.

I asked the Princess to describe Rudolf to me.

'You could see he was a kind person not only outwardly but his soul was also kind, generous, as a true artist, giving to his audience.

'The first thing I noticed about Rudolf was his mouth, not his eyes, which are the usual thing to see and examine when one first meets someone. It was extraordinary, wide, misshapen and fascinating.

'He was always posing or seemed to be, with his head in profile to the left or right, as an artist used to performing continuously to his audience would do. He gave the appearance of someone trying to stand taller or appear taller. I am quite tall and felt that he was trying to raise himself.'

There is another story.

Princess Michael and her husband were in Venice. 'I adore Venice, it is my bolthole,' she told me. They stopped near a bridge to look at a children's clothes shop. Her daughter was at this time about six months old. 'My husband fell in love with a beautiful blue spotted dress in the window. But it was for a six year old and our daughter was so small then. My husband was insistent; he thought it was so pretty.

'As we were looking at the dress in the window, I was goosed! Rudolf was walking past and he goosed me. It was very funny. From that moment on, when my daughter reached three years old and as a tall child she was able to wear this beautiful dress, it became known as "the Nureyev dress".'

This story seemed to me to epitomise Rudolf: he was not only defiant of protocol, incredibly cheeky and irreverent, but also used to using a gesture rather than words. As Princess Michael said, she did not know Rudolf that well at all and had only met him on a few occasions.

This action really did speak louder than a thousand words.

Now I wanted to speak to Violette Verdy, the person who had put me in touch with Robert and had reunited Robert and Rudi in 1980.

I asked Violette to start at the beginning with how she first met Rudolf.

'I first saw him in Paris with the Marquis de Cuevas Ballet company. This was just after he had defected. He was dancing *Swan Lake* and Bluebird from *The Sleeping Beauty*. I cannot remember who was with me, but we both went backstage afterwards to see him.

'He was incredible to watch. He was both male and female in his sexiness and when he danced *Swan Lake*, you know, he became a swan. It was if he had to be a swan in order to portray the man who had fallen in love with one. It was simply wonderful to watch.'

I couldn't find any information on their dancing partnership and where Rudi and Violette had appeared together so I asked her about this.

'This is what is so incredible: we never ever danced together. For the Margot Fonteyn Gala at Covent Garden in the '60s, Rudolf had chosen two ballerinas that he wanted to partner and I was one of them. But I was in Russia with New York City Ballet when the gala was performed. I was married at the time to Colin Clarke, Kenneth Clarke's brother, you know, the MP.

'We spent all that time as friends, never having danced together. So, one time when we were warming up on stage before a performance, we were just in our practice clothes. We grabbed each other and danced together but with no audience,' recounts Violette.

I wanted to know how they had become so close over the years and what Violette had thought Rudolf was really like.

'He was primitive, untamed. He did everything instinctively, almost barbarously. He was never ever duped and he was never a victim.'

Violette continued, 'You know, it was like he was in a race, he had to do everything, and really everything, as soon as he could. Looking back, it was as if he knew he hadn't got a lot of time, even in the '60s. He died so young and can you imagine what he would have gone on to achieve as a teacher and choreographer? It would have been incredible.

'Rudolf was all about power. He was more than an interpreter. He was intriguing and so alluring. He learned everything by necessity very quickly and he was so multi-talented.'

It is very hard not to smile with Violette at all these memories. She is such a gentle person to talk to and cares so passionately about ballet and dance. Her accent takes you to a softer, more caring world.

I asked Violette how well she had known Margot.

'Margot was a goddess. She was a wonderful friend and again someone taken away before their time by dreadful illness. We were all brought up together and danced together, so knew each other very well. Ballet was a small world then.

'Rudolf, Margot and I used to go to Hector's studio for class. Rudolf adored Hector. This was in New York and the studio was above the nightclub Studio 54. It was crazy being above that club. We had these wonderful private classes. Whenever Rudi and Margot landed anywhere in the world they would find their favourite person and head straight for class with them,' said Violette.

I had read that Rudi and Violette had talked about Margot, and from that it seemed that Rudi had told Violette that he had slept with Margot. But when I asked Violette about this, she was almost shocked or taken aback.

'I never asked Rudolf about Margot. I couldn't. It wasn't something that I would ever ask. He had told me that he had slept with women but that they, the affairs, took too long.'

I knew that Bill Akers had known Margot for years and I was certain that he would be able to tell me more about this legendary friendship.

'We were on tour, in Paris, playing the huge sports arena, Palais des Sports. We had this small cut-out cross for *Giselle*, which looked fine everywhere else, but it did disappear in that huge stadium. Rudi took one look at it and said, "Darling, you must get me a bigger cross. Ask the Paris Opéra, they will let you have something, they love me."

'Well, they had the same sort of cross for *Giselle* as we did and one huge cross from *Spartacus* which I took back with me to the Palais des Sports.

'Margot came onto the stage area, took one look at this enormous cross and said to me, "Bill, darling, I know he is famous but he's not Atlas." We had such a giggle about that. Then of course Rudi turned up with Erik and started to add embellishment after embellishment to the solos for Albrecht. It was getting ludicrous and Erik said that he shouldn't, but Rudi said that the French loved him, adored him, and he wanted to do the embellishments, the extra steps. Margot just said, "No, Rudi", and that was the end of it. He did not do them.

'You see I think he knew that he had so much to learn. So when Margot said no, he respected that.

'It was like our daily spats. He craved the discipline. Because that was what he was used to. He was brought up on such strict discipline at home at the Kirov. In the West, very few people gave it to him. He needed you to shout back at him and say no to him. Just like Margot did,' Bill recalled.

'You also have to remember how famous they were. They attracted huge stars and celebrities wherever they went. One night in Paris, I was attending to one of Margot's legs. She had a slight injury to her "monkey muscle" or Achilles tendon. I always acted as a physio for her when we were on tour. Anyway, we were in this dreadful dressing-room, rather like a locker-room, when there was a knock at the makeshift doorway. I checked with Margot then went to see who it was. Standing in the doorway was this incredibly beautiful woman. She was wearing a white trousersuit, which was most unusual in those days, and a trilby hat with a small veil over her face, and, of course, I realised that this was Marlene Dietrich.

'She came in to see Margot and it turned out that they were old friends. Dietrich told Margot how she looked so young on stage, how wonderful she looked, and asked how did she manage it?

'Margot pointed to me and said, "Bill does my lighting, that is how I look so good."

'Dietrich said, "He fixes your legs and he lights you, maybe we should both buy him!"

'After Tito, Margot's husband, was shot, Margot did not have an escort and so in Australia she used to ask me to organise her parties, her wine lists, the food and the venues. I was happy to do this. After all, we had known each other so long.

'Now I want to get rid of one rumour once and for all. I was very cross when one of the newspapers phoned me to ask me to comment about one of the books and the story that Margot had been pregnant. It had implied that the child would have been Rudolf's. Impossible,

I said. But I was very irritated and when I was back in the house I remembered that, yes, I did know about this and could sort it out once and for all.

'Margot always used to say to me that there was to be no expense spared for her parties, they had to be perfect. This particular party was taking place before we were due to fly off to perform for Imelda Marcos, who was a great friend of Margot's. The party was in Canberra at the Chanticleer.

'There were 21 of us. I was sitting on Margot's right and Vera Volkova was on her left. Vera Volkova was Erik Bruhn's teacher, a Russian émigrée who had set up a highly influential and respected school in England and also taught Rudolf.

'Sitting beside Vera was Frances Towers, and Roger sat beside me. Frances was Margot's dresser. She was a small apple-cheeked lady whom Margot adored, and she always stipulated in her contract that Frances had to be her dresser in Australia. Funnily enough, Frances and Margot seemed to be the only ones who could understand what Tito was saying after he had been shot, though to be honest with you I don't know that Frances could, but she was quite happy to just sit talking to him and chattering away.

'During the meal, Margot whispered to me to see if I thought it was going well. I reassured her that it was a great success and I asked her something that I had always meant to ask her but the moment always passed.

'"Margot, who designed your style? You do not do great leaps or arabesques like the Russian stars. It obviously was not Bobby Helpmann as it would be more flamboyant. You are always so arté and beautifully placed."

'Margot replied, "I am sorry to disillusion you but it was all I could ever do and as the public seemed to like it, I kept doing it."

'At the end of this answer we had both caught the tail-end of Frances and Vera's conversation and Margot asked them what they had been talking about.

'Vera looked slightly embarrassed and then said in that way that only women can to each other, "We were saying what a terrible tragedy it was that you never had Tito's child before his accident."

'There was a pause. Then Margot replied, "Frances, Vera, Tito knew long before we were married that I could never have anybody's child."

'I always took this to mean that she could not have children and that was the end of that. So, as for any abortions or pregnancies with Rudi or anyone else, it just was not on the cards.' Bill Akers is very firm about this, adding, 'And, I have witnesses to this conversation!'

'You know, Rudi and Margot were the very best of friends. Their friendship transcended simple friendship, it was far more than that. But as for there being anything sexual, that is just rubbish.'

The man who learned from Margot Fonteyn and had taught himself so much was about to teach me too.

It was a very hot and humid London evening. There was no air-conditioning in the Coliseum backstage at that time and everyone suffered, audience and performers alike.

I was laden with shopping, plastic carrier bags, handbag and internal mail as I walked past the open door to the number-one dressing-room. I saw that Rudolf was in there, said "Hi" and went straight in.

I sat down and asked him how he was. This was, after all, how I would behave with any member of a company, be they actor, dancer, singer or musician. It was unusual for us to meet like this, though, as our evening rendezvous would normally be on stage.

Whenever I saw him sitting alone in his dressing-room I thought how lonely or alone he seemed. This was a different feeling to the one you sense when an artist is preparing and wants the peace and quiet of their dressing-room. Rudi could be on tour with a large company but would still seem completely by himself.

He was sitting bare-chested, putting on the traditionally heavy ballet make-up. This was even more crucial in a house the size of the Coliseum as it was needed in order for your face to be 'read' or seen throughout the theatre.

I hope that I did not look like a gauche schoolgirl with my shopping balanced on my lap, watching every single move of the panstick, but I have an awful feeling that this was exactly what I did look like.

He smiled at me and waited for whatever great pronouncement I was going to make. I didn't really have anything to say, though, I was just being friendly.

The weather is always safe in a conversation. The heat really was awful and I did not have to dance in it. As the Coliseum did not have any air conditioning, I knew the audience would suffer as well. When I started to commiserate with him, Rudolf told me a story about the Coliseum and its architecture. I was transfixed. I had worked there for years but had not heard any of this before and here I was hearing it from Rudolf Nureyev.

It was an amazing tale, embellished with a thick accent and much twinkling of the eyes, and punctuated with jabs and blending of panstick, checking of profile and sucking-in of cheeks.

'You know the blue panels in the roof?' He was talking to me through the dressing-room mirror, watching my reaction.

'Above the audience.'

I nodded to his mirrored reflection. I pictured the huge turquoise 'ruched' triangular panels high above the heads of everyone, ending in a 'lantern' that led to the famous Coliseum ball on top of the dome.

There was a long pause whilst thick black lines were placed down his nose for shading. 'During Victorian times they opened grilles just beneath these in the interval, to let the air in.'

I was riveted, as white was now being applied to his chiselled cheekbones and black shaded in a triangle underneath.

'When they were opened, everyone's hats and programmes flew up in the air.' The tale finishes with a flourish of the arm in the air, 'Like this', and a roar of laughter.

It was a wonderful vision. I was left grinning like an idiot, sitting staring in the mirror at him with this huge theatrical expression, wide-eyed, posed, lips pouted and his arm in the air.

I believe that he was actually there in his mind, grabbing for a top hat that had deserted him in the updraught.

He could see it and touch it, and so could I.

CHAPTER FOUR

Raspberries

The large grey French 'poodle' with ludicrous floppy ears and a red bow tie left the stage and pretended to lift its leg against a piece of scenery. We all laughed conspiratorially. The magic was gone in an instant, as the poodle stepped out of his all-in-one suit to reveal a ballet dancer, glossy with sweat and now nearly naked bar painted whiskers and a black splodge on his nose.

It was 1982, I was here for my second Nureyev Festival and the second ballet company were rehearsing. We were watching *La Boutique Fantasque,* a pantomime of a piece with its clear jokes and fun.

I was pleased to be back for a second Nureyev Festival season. Actually, it was much more than that. I was hugely excited.

There were two ballet companies this year and we had started a week earlier with Zurich Ballet again. This time they performed two ballets that were new to me: the wonderful moody *Manfred* – choreographed and created by Nureyev and based on Goethe's epic poem *Manfred* – and *Western Symphony*. *Manfred* was a dark brooding piece with music by Tchaikovsky. It was created by Rudolf to show off his physicality and it astounded the critics when this production was first premiered in 1979 at the Palais des Sports in Paris. Rudolf had certainly set himself a challenge: despite the fact that he was 'in decline', the role lasted over one hour on stage.

Next was the fun and exuberance of the 'cowboy' ballet. *Western Symphony* was performed to the music of Aaron Copeland and was full of toe-tapping energy, cowgirls, saloon girls and cowboys, with 'yee hah's all the way through.

Work between the seasons for me had been spasmodic; although the country was beginning to show signs of recovery after the recession, there was also general unrest, shown clearly in the Brixton riots of 1981. There wasn't a lot of work around in the theatre, with long gaps between contracts. Tough times. So it was good to be back at the Coliseum. I always felt at home there, having worked on and off in that theatre for nearly ten years. In addition, it was also nice to have been asked to work on something for a second time. I had been devastated not to be able to accept an invitation to work the 1981 season – the luck of the draw for a freelance meant that I had accepted work elsewhere that year. I had had to resign myself to missing a summer in London with Nureyev, but now the fact that I had been asked again in 1982 reassured me that they must have been happy with my work first time round. I ignored the cynical little voice inside saying that maybe it was just a case of better the devil you know.

When I thought back to it now, most of the first Nureyev Festival had a warm rosy glow around it. I remembered the crowds, the fun company, the flowers, the applause, and, yes, of course, a few moments of angst and confrontation, but somehow the memories all had a kind of cosy feeling about them. I had carefully erased the days of no communication and the tension that I must have experienced. I used to compare the Nureyev Festivals with all their various components – international ballet companies, orchestras and Nureyev – to running the UN. But now, in 1982, I dismissed such thoughts. I was back in the world of entrechats, fouettés, port de bras, battements and attitude, of the balletic kind, not the twenty-first century kind, and was beginning to understand what these mysterious directions and descriptions for dancers meant.

I enjoyed watching the unfamiliar ballets and also loved listening to the shopping and sightseeing tales from the visiting companies. Being on tour with a show – whether as a dancer, actor, singer or part of the crew – is unlike any other experience, I think. And there are points of similarity in what you experience whether you are the star or a lowly assistant stage manager.

It is a lonely and expensive business to work away from home and have time on your hands. You can stay in your hotel room or your 'digs', the cheapest accommodation that you can suffer and afford, or you can spend your time walking around the town or city trying not to spend money. Which is really impossible!

When hotels, digs and retail therapy failed, the allure of a quiet dressing-room, with just the bumps, echoes and ghosts of an empty theatre, would often win the day for me. I chose this option when I wanted a good long read. It worked: over the years, those quiet hours allowed me to work through Dostoyevsky, Tolstoy, Chekhov and Stendhal. They were good touring companions.

However tedious touring sometimes seemed, I always felt excited about visiting new cities and meeting new people. And there would also often be familiar faces about. We had some 'camp followers', the weird families that followed the various companies out on the road. In every town and city the same families would loiter outside, mum, dad and the rather bewildered-looking children hovering at the stage door to collect autographs. I wondered if they ever noticed all the 'Robert Redford's signed by our crew and also wondered how they managed to afford to do this week after week. I just couldn't work it out.

Bill Akers has a fan letter to Rudolf from an American woman who followed him all around the world on their tours. From the letter it would appear that Rudolf had replied to one of her previous attempts to contact him. I was fascinated to know how people managed their lives around this compulsion to see their idols everywhere they went. I was also curious to hear that at this stage in Nureyev's career he had been inclined to correspond with a woman.

Touring was all about the performance, but it was also about affairs, long train journeys, unrequited love and tears on the last night. It was normal to have two sets of rooming lists on tour with some companies. The accurate list was for internal use but another one was kept for the benefit of husbands, wives, lovers and partners. One was published and the other kept very much under wraps. This was clearly a disaster waiting to happen, especially if someone's partner turned up to pay a surprise visit. There was also the nightmare when a mother phoned 'just to say hello' but couldn't find her offspring and neither could I as they had changed rooms without warning.

While on tour, you learn the stories, traditions, games and people that make up the world of theatre. There are patterns that never change. Every Sunday, you arrive in a strange town and work out your way to the new theatre. You can see the theatre but the traffic system takes you on a tour of the town. Then comes the relief of seeing the unmistakable sight of the 6 ft 7 in. tall props master striding his way back from 'the office', the nearest pub, to the theatre, so you know you are getting close.

You also learn about survival away from home and how to keep your sanity. Whilst I was shopping till I dropped around the UK, Rudolf Nureyev watched *I Love Lucy* re-runs. *Chacun à son goût*. We all had our own ways of coping out on tour.

In 1982, we soon settled into a daily routine with the ballet companies. The only change to the rhythm of class, rehearsals, the ritual gathering of flowers, the outstanding curtain calls and the hordes of fans at the stage door came with the change of companies at the weekend. After the Saturday performance, it was out with the old and in with the new – a job that lasted through the night. Then came the Sunday load-in, when huge wagons arrived to disgorge their contents through the dock doors (the scenic doors) of the theatre.

Around the world every Sunday, in each and every large touring house theatre, this first day is being repeated. It was always a relief for me when the load-in was completed. It meant we were getting nearer to the show. And this time a company I had not worked with before, Ballet Théâtre Français de Nancy, were to introduce me to the wide variations of the work of Diaghilev – *Petrouchka*, *Le Spectre de la Rose* and *L'Après-midi d'un Faune* – that Rudolf had made his own.

As ever, the crew had been eyeing up the new influx, working out who spoke English, who was the boss and, probably more realistically, who were going to be good drinking partners for the week. Groups of men huddled around large plans on the stage whilst the overhead lighting bars were lowered in, ready to put on any lanterns required for the new show. Stagehands showed off the stage and wings of this magnificent theatre designed by Frank Matcham to their new colleagues for the week to come, in a way that displayed a sense of ownership. We all took pride in the wonderful auditorium and sheer scale of the theatre. There was a sense of urgency, too, about making sure everything was exactly right for the important Nureyev Festival. Of course, everyone tried their best for all the shows we were involved with, but these seasons with Nureyev were a sell-out and came with the greatest critic of all, Rudolf himself.

In a grand show of cockney machismo, some of the Coliseum crew started running the 30-foot flats one-handed at fantastic speeds across the stage. If you got the purchase point exactly right on the edge of one of these trembling monsters, you could cross the stage in seconds instead of sedately 'running' (another strange theatre term when the meaning is just moving) the flat across the stage with one person on either edge. If you got your hand position even a millimetre out, the flat would go nowhere other than to nosedive onto the floor, sending a cloud of dust everywhere to the accompaniment of cheers and jeers. This performance was meant to impress and it did. It was a thrilling display of territorial marking and a twentieth-century version of throwing down the gauntlet.

Round two of this contest was done with a flick of the wrist, and only the most foolhardy risked the taunting of their peers when they failed. In order to build a wall of scenic flats, the flats had to be joined together. They were carefully positioned edge to edge and they had to be fastened at at least one of their edges. The fastening was the trick that brought many a stagehand to his knees in exasperation.

Taking the long piece of sash rope, which is attached to the top of one of the flats, in their hand, they attempted to fasten it by cleating it to another flat, with a whip-like action from one flat to another, to secure them solidly in a zig-zag fastening. Usually this ended in complete failure to roars of laughter from the assembled audience. If done when no one else was looking, then, of course, it always worked in three swift flicks of the wrist.

Unwieldy wicker baskets and rail after rail of costumes were struggled with up and down the impossible Victorian staircases of the Coliseum. Wigs, make-up boxes and shoes in labelled and marked white canvas bags, like schoolchildren's at boarding school, were piled up in the corridors waiting to be placed in dressing-rooms for the week.

I tried to make myself look busy and showed people the dressing-rooms, the stage or the canteen as requested. And to stave off boredom I would volunteer to run around the dressing-rooms with name cards. Often I simply sat in the office waiting for the next question, reading the Sunday papers and listening to ominous crashes over the Tannoy. I would always be amazed that when I looked back at the stage, what had been a black open space just a few hours ago now had a colourful floor cloth and the wings had disappeared behind packs of tall scenic flats.

Sometimes, when I returned from some mission to the top of the building and the hidden dressing-rooms far away from the stage, the whole place would be deserted. I had missed the mandatory introductory guide to the stage-door pub, an essential part of any touring technicians' guide to the Coliseum, so I was on my own. I hated it when that happened. There was just the sound of an empty theatre to keep me company whilst I ploughed through the rest of the papers and a stale sandwich.

Our afternoon was spent lighting the new ballet, hanging cloths, checking their positions and hanging heights – seeing just how far they had to be flown in to look perfect. It was a relaxed time, with people wandering around the stage aping dancers or personalities, whilst standing in the correct place for the lights.

It was a change for me to be out in the stalls rather than walking the positions on the stage. I loved to share touring stories about cities around the world and there are certain names or places that unite everyone: La Fenice in Venice and the scenery arriving by gondola, or the organisational wonder at all the theatres in Vienna. In Vienna you could leave a box with your name and the theatre on it in your dressing-room and, rather than drag it by taxi across to the next theatre you were playing in, it would miraculously turn up in the right place at the right time, seemingly all by itself.

We shared theatre ghost stories and delighted in the looks on the faces of the visitors as we told them all the ones we knew about the Coliseum. I recounted my experience with Mrs White, the housekeeper, or rather her ghost. Allegedly, she met an untimely end and wasn't discovered for a while. The story was that drink had been involved and she had fallen down some stairs. One night I was photocopying during a lighting session for *The Ring*. Probably something exotic, like the 'Dragon' plot, showing the moves of the dragon, how high it went, how often and the length between the cues. We also had 'Ring' plots, 'Tarnhelm' plots, 'Nothung' plots, anything to help the uninitiated survive their first encounter with any part of *The Ring*, with its arcane names for swords, magic crowns and the cast who used them.

The fireman, who was doing his rounds, came in to see who was working. Just as he entered the room, however, it went icy cold and all the lights blew. I had never been so scared and we took off. We ran through the stalls promenade and turned a sharp right into the stalls. We were both terrified and literally shaking. We told everyone what had happened, as we had made quite an entrance. Everyone calmly pointed out that we had been in the exact spot where her body had been found.

This was a great spooky story to tell people whilst sitting in the dark in a huge theatre. When I told Rudi about this experience, though, he laughed and asked me to remember to 'introduce me to Mrs White!' I think that he thought I was joking. Everyone else had to look behind them after hearing it.

I also told the story about the 'King's Car'. There used to be a 'railway', well, more like an electric tram, that ran from the royal entrance in St Martin's Lane to the royal box. This was when the royal box was situated where the sound and light control rooms are now. This 'car' was built especially for King Edward VII, but on its very first day in service it failed and the King had to walk. The royal loo used to be where the Stalls Bar is now.

We talked about Sergei Diaghilev too. The Coliseum had a great history of ballet stretching back well before Fonteyn and Nureyev, and Diaghilev featured prominently. I remembered a ballet and opera gala where a magnificent front-cloth had arrived complete with security guards and minders. This was the wonderful Picasso front cloth for *Le Train Bleu*.

Sir Oswald Stoll, who used to own the Coliseum when it was a variety house, had heard that the Diaghilev Ballet Company was stuck in France having completed a tour, and were basically starving. They had made their way there from England during the First World War. Stoll sent them an advance and they returned to England in 1918 to top the bill with various pieces. In the company at the time were such stars as the ballerina Nijinska, Serge Lifar, George Balanchine and Ninette de Valois. Stoll became concerned, though, as they were so popular that people were turning up just to see the ballet and then leaving before the 'rubbish' started. As a result, he moved the company to the Alhambra Theatre. This was a large theatre on the south end of Leicester Square. In their place at the Coliseum he staged a skit by J.M. Barrie called *The Truth about the Russian dancers: showing how they love, how they marry, how they are made and how they die and live happily ever after*. The irony of hearing about this piece from a friend whilst writing about Nureyev was not lost on me. This one-acter starred Karsavina.

Roger Myers remembers, 'One day I had to give Rudolf the bad news that Tamara Karsavina, the star of Ballets Russes, was very ill and in a nursing home.'

Karsavina had danced with Nijinsky and had said of Rudi's lover Erik Bruhn that, 'Erik is certainly a wonderful dancer but he lacks Nureyev's nerve.'

'She didn't have a lot of money and people were very concerned. Rudi said, "She was a wonderful dancer. Tell them I will pay for everything; you tell them, Roger." Which of course I did, and as far as I know he did pay for everything for her.' Karsavina died in 1979.

The Diaghilev Company returned to the Coliseum in 1924 and one of the ballets that they presented then was *La Boutique Fantasque*. It was a good feeling to be working on something that had so much to do with this theatre.

A few weeks prior to the 1982 season, I had been working from the Victor Hochhauser offices in Holland Park Avenue. The offices were in a large house, in a lovely part of London. I was based with a colleague in the basement looking out to a beautiful garden. We were sifting through all the letters from extras or supers (supernumeraries) who had heard on the grapevine or seen advertised well in advance that we were doing *Petrouchka* and knew that we would need them.

It was fairly easy to work through the applications as most of them had appeared in the Nureyev Festivals in *Petrouchka* in the seasons before. With a fairly small repertoire of ballets it was quite usual for the same ballets to come round each year but with different companies who had their own productions. There would be subtle variations with different scenery, designs and choreography.

We then moved to the Coliseum for the auditions and people and bodies were matched to the frocks. This was a fun type of audition. Not the heart-rending slog of rejection that dancers, singers and actors usually go through: queuing for hours then standing on a bare stage or a strange set staring into the darkness of the auditorium. Just how many times can you listen to 'Memory' from *Cats*? There was still a sense of anxiety, though. All these people were desperate to be part of the season in order to work with, be near and be able to tell everyone about Nureyev.

Measurements, names, addresses, Equity numbers, rehearsal calls and chat were the order of the day for those who were chosen. I took these dancers through dressing-room lists and signing-in lists. Some sneaked in cameras just in case they got a chance to take a photo. There was a tremendous buzz. This was a great new family to work with for the season.

Once the actors, supers and extras were sorted, then, suddenly, we were into the season proper. On the Monday after Zurich Ballet had left, our first day with Ballet Théâtre Français de Nancy, just as we were about to progress with the rehearsals, we were diverted by a voice calling to us from the black hole of the auditorium. The florists were hanging floral bowers and swags on the front of the royal box. With perfect timing, we had just turned out the house lights in the auditorium and they could not see. Of course, we had lights on stage, but as we were about to drop the curtain, they would have no light at all. At least this time it was not the cleaners, who usually arrived to vacuum at that most crucial moment: when there are no lights and the atmosphere requires silence.

The smell from the flowers, even on stage, was overwhelming. I wondered how anyone could sit inches away from that potent heady smell even for five minutes, let alone two hours of ballet. The florists were quick to request that we set up a working light for them in the box, so they could continue. One of our electricians was tasked with putting a 'stand' up there, shorthand for a light on a stand. He dutifully returned with a music stand and, with a cheerful smile, asked where we would like it. This was not the powerful spotlight that we had hoped for. Our chief electrician looked on in dismay, shook his head and muttered actually quite loudly, 'brain power of a retarded J cloth'. We all sniggered like kids.

Bill Akers had a good time with Rudi on the subject of boxes, lights and sight lines.

'We were doing *Sleeping Beauty* in Perth. Rudi came onto the stage one day wearing that full-length fur coat and that hat that fell over his left shoulder. He shouted "Honey darling!" He did eventually stop calling me this and it became a very Russian "Beel" for Bill. I joked back that "the world stops for Mr Nureyev".

'The theatre we were in had some strangely positioned boxes for the audience on each side, and Rudi had spotted this and told me to, "Take them down, get rid of them". I laughed and said that I could do many things, but demolishing interiors of theatres wasn't one of them. He carried on, "They are bad, no one can see. Who sits there?" I explained that the theatre management thought that they were rather good for the visually impaired or blind people. He fell on the floor in hysterics. His black Russian humour really was strange sometimes. He was actually crying with laughter. "You Australians look after everyone," he gasped. His humour could be very morbid.'

Having seen that our royal box problem was over, I was about to raise myself to my full height and shout the predictable line, 'Stand by, please', when I spotted a group huddled around an object downstage centre. It looked familiar.

A group of property staff and electricians stood with their hands in their pockets, or holding rolled-up prop sheets like scrolls, pencils behind ears, rocking on their heels. They were standing round a desk and a debate was in progress.

Clearly this was no ordinary desk. If it had been an ordinary desk, it would be a piece of furniture and therefore the responsibility of the props staff. This desk was special because it had a lamp on it, which meant there was a possibility of it being the responsibility of the electrics department.

These debates could run for hours, with phrases like 'customs and practice' and 'I have done this for years and it is always electrics, ask Charlie' floating across the stage. I had got used to keeping a low profile during these satellite meetings of the Oxbridge philosophical debating society.

Visiting company technicians stood around looking bemused at the high art and practice of a union house, whose members have been successfully trained in canteen philosophy. I watched from the prompt corner, keeping a wary eye open for Rudi, who was due any moment. As one of the props staff sauntered off the stage and into the wings muttering, 'Give me strength', I gathered they had solved this million-pound question. Sure enough, a beleaguered-looking electrician solemnly carried the offending desk with lamp off stage.

It was going to be a very long day.

The florists were happy and we were now in our usual position of standing by for the stand-by: we were all ready but nothing happened, yet we all had to be there. A sound operator called it 'hurry-up-and-wait syndrome'. You are all waiting for each other sometimes, the orchestra waiting for the dancers or vice versa and there is often the frustration of someone asking for a few more minutes then not telling you that they are ready. Waiting on a large, brightly lit stage, people began to get fidgety and to lose patience, until we finally started.

We began with *La Boutique Fantasque* and Rudolf did not appear in this.

It was a little strange, no clogs, no Thermos flask, no towel, no watch.

I was by myself in the prompt corner, no Nureyev. I was expecting him to be there, warming up ready for the first ballet, but as he wasn't appearing in it, I was on my own.

The first rehearsal of *La Boutique Fantasque* was fun and fast. There were poodles, toys, children and that music that I recognised but had not realised was also a ballet. Crowds of stagehands stood in the wings watching young French ballerinas and dreaming. No, they were lusting. I really enjoyed that ballet and ended each performance with a smile.

We stopped and took a break to change the set from *Boutique* to *Petrouchka*. This was out of sequence from the show's running order, as *Petrouchka* was the last ballet to be performed each night.

I went to the number-one dressing-room and knocked. No reaction. I couldn't believe that we were going to go through all this again. I knocked again, said my name and opened the door.

I was greeted by a half-smile. He was merely changing into his warm-up gear. He asked me how it was going, how long he had and just as I was leaving, 'What have you been up to?' in that wonderful accent. With that soft voice, he seemed gentle, almost shy.

I asked him if he wanted to come and check the *Petrouchka* inset. This inset was a flat through which he had to fall each night. The hole he pretended to make in the flat was covered with new paper for each performance. He said that he would leave it to me.

I asked him how much longer he needed, just for badness, to see what his reaction would be and said, 'No worries, wave at me in the prompt corner when you are ready.' He wouldn't, though; I would have to guess by the murmur that would fly through the wings.

I decided not to risk being sidetracked by extras and others in the wings on my way to check the flat, and, instead, walked round the back of the Coliseum stage via the infamously named back passage. Painted the same institutional green and cream as the old dressing-rooms, it wasn't an easy route. After a straight stretch you came up against a seemingly impenetrable wall and had to do a 90-degree right turn. It was just about wide enough for two of you to pass, avoiding caged-in belching hot pipes. At some point in time, someone had carefully painted a red line to show you where to walk as you squeezed through this narrow corridor and round its blind corners to stage left.

I found the huge 30-foot white flat with the paper carefully pasted over the bottom section. This flat was a piece of scenery to the stage crew, who were responsible for putting it in place, but it was a member of the props staff who had to put the paper over it.

After I was sure that everything was OK, I strolled across the stage behind the house curtain. The extras and supers were milling around, wanting to stay and watch Rudolf. For some, this would be their first opportunity to see him; others had worked with him before, but they were still agog. A lovely older actor used to bring in handmade chocolates on matinée days to keep everyone going and one of the female extras tried every night to speak to Rudolf. She wanted to give him healing on his ankle, which had a spur, a bony growth that gave him a lot of pain. She was distressed that for yet another year she had failed to meet him. But she would crouch resolutely near the prompt corner, sending out her thoughts to him as he danced. Maybe it helped.

One of the visiting company asked me, 'How much longer is Rudi going to be?' I had no idea but said that I would go and check in a minute or two.

At such times I had a choice whether to rehearse the scene changes without Rudi, as the orchestra was in the pit and ready, or to wait for him and start from the beginning. It was a real gamble with *Petrouchka*. If we did start with scene changes, Rudi would invariably come on to the stage and ask, 'What are you doing? Why can't we start?'

Rudolf arrived in the wings without my prompting and once we started rehearsing, it was fast and *Petrouchka* flew by. Then, it was on to *Le Spectre de la Rose,* and *L'Après-midi d'un Faune*. There were no problems and the rehearsals passed quickly.

I left the sunny feel of the main stage to return to my dark hideaway of the stage manager's desk. I was in a bit of a quandary as to what to do now. It was an odd time to finish and we had a spare hour before Rudolf would have usually started his warm-up. As he didn't appear in *Boutique*, I was not sure what he would require and when; a barre in the wings was ready, though, for any eventuality.

As I sat pondering this problem, a posse of people came through the pass door: promoters, directors of the ballet company and 'suits' from the theatre.

There was to be a party for the company that night and they needed to know if Rudolf would come. I had not seen Robert recently so I assumed he was away or at home. There was an enormous amount of indecision and a lot of turned backs. The posse decided to leave. But then one of them asked, beautifully timed so that I really did not have an escape route, if I would check with

Rudolf if he would be at the party and which guests he would be taking. This request was imparted so casually that you would think it was the easiest thing in the world to do and that they were just being incredibly grand or lazy. I knew by now, however, that this performance disguised a 'not for all the tea in China' deep fear of confronting Nureyev with anything, including even a simple invitation. I was surprised that people in their position found him so daunting and such a challenge, but maybe they had learned from bitter experience.

I said I would try for them and then escaped for a while to breathe the 'fresh air' of Bedfordbury. I wandered off towards Covent Garden market via the Scottish Wool Merchant, the beautiful scientific instrument shop and the quaint '80s gift boutiques that had sprung up all around. I thought about going round the National Portrait Gallery, but the weather was too nice. I opted for strolling round the lanes, past The Lamb and Flag and up to Covent Garden. I stopped to watch the world go by, just enjoying being there in London in the high summer.

But you can have too much of tumblers, magicians and crowds. The noise from the Hard Rock Café was now addling my brain and I headed off for a night of pure fantasy and a dream that it wouldn't have occurred to me might ever happen: working again on the Nureyev Festival. I could not have been happier. I felt sunny and relaxed as I meandered back.

The crew were all sitting on the low wall opposite the stage door, taking in the rays. I waved and disappeared into the cool green and cream world beyond the stage door. There were no messages for me and no post, so I headed off down to the world downstairs.

There, all was serenity and calm.

A few moments later, as I was walking quietly down the wings, I saw a solitary ballet dancer rehearsing by herself in the middle of the stage to an empty auditorium. She was practising 'spotting'. She made eye contact with a specific point somewhere in the auditorium – at Sadler's Wells there was a red light that the dancers used for this purpose, at the Coliseum there was a wide choice – fixing herself for her turns so that she did not get dizzy. Over and over again she did this and I knew that she, like all of the dancers, would rehearse every day for eight hours and then perform that night. There was a great story going round once about one of the corps de ballet in London Festival Ballet. She had a pedometer fitted for a matinée and evening performance of *Swan Lake* and after the two shows it allegedly registered 17 miles. Just for one day. I cannot imagine doing a near marathon even once and here they were, and still are, doing one and sometimes two a week.

However much they rehearsed and strove for perfection, though, you should always expect the unexpected even from the greatest dancers. Bill Akers has a story that illustrates this perfectly.

'We were at the O'Keefe Center in Canada [now called the Hummingbird Center for the Performing Arts], doing *Sleeping Beauty*. Jack Lanchbery was conducting and Rudi entered for his big solo. He came on and did this big preparation, then a jump, then a double cabriole, and then there was the most almighty thump. He just dropped from about four feet in the air with such a bang, landing smack on his bottom. I was horrified and wondered what on earth he would do now. He got up with a black thunderous face. The orchestra had stopped playing. He held his finger in the air and smiled, as if to say to the audience, "Now, just wait. Not one single word." I took a photo of this as his smile said "Just you wait and see." Jack Lanchbery was just standing there in the pit waiting to see what happened, and Rudi walked off the stage.

'The audience was sitting in stunned silence. This moment seemed to go on for hours. It was a really unusual situation as no announcement was made and there was no way of knowing what was going to happen next.

'Suddenly, all we could hear was this terrible scratching and pawing going on in the rosin tray over on the other side of the stage in the wings. You could hear Rudolf walk round the back of the stage and then he entered again. It was worth the wait for all of us. He prepared, and then proceeded to do the most amazing variation, something I am never likely to see again. It was breathtaking. The audience went wild. He did it to prove that he was Nureyev.

'His dedication was so strong. Lupe Serrano summed him up one day when she was to partner him in *Diana and Actaeon*. She was late arriving at the theatre and Rudolf was getting fretful. He sent me to find her. I had no idea if she was even in the building. She had only given birth a couple of weeks earlier. I found her in the corridor, swearing and cursing about being held up at the airport. She changed in minutes. She was a lovely woman.

'Walking down the wings, she stopped and watched Rudi rehearsing. She turned to me and said, "There he is busting his balls and no one gives a fuck, do they, no audience. But you just watch him when there is."'

I asked Bill more about this dedication to his performance.

'We were doing *Giselle*. As I mentioned before, his Albrecht was a deep and powerful performance of sheer artistry and acting. On the opening night he came running on in Act 2, trying to find Giselle, and he was looking everywhere, running backwards and forwards. I was watching this intently and I found myself joining in this "looking".

'He was looking and I was looking back. I told myself to get a grip, for heaven's sake. I had been trained not to catch anyone's eye on the stage whilst they were performing and here I was joining in from the wings. The curtain calls were amazing that night. The audience nearly pulled the house down.

'The next night I made a determined effort not to look at him. He came screaming off and was abusing me, I had no idea what was the matter.'

'"Pig, *pisstushka*. Where were you? I was looking and you did not help me."

'I had no idea he had wanted me to help him, so I apologised to him, but I was saddled with this routine every single night. It really became quite a bore.'

I settled into the office and listened to the sounds of the theatre waking up over the Tannoy. My mind was half on the task of when to ask Rudolf about the party: before or during the show. Timing, it was all in the timing. The interconnecting door between the stage management office and the master carpenter's office opened bang on cue as always, just as I was changing out of my T-shirt and jeans. There was no point in false modesty as this had happened nightly for the past ten years or so and it was never intentional, though sometimes it felt like it was. I had to just stand there and listen to their query or comment with a resigned expression.

The stage management office was stuffy and overlit after the sunlight of Covent Garden. I used to stumble mole-like out of the safety of the lit world into a dark forest of monstrously high scenery. I always tripped over something – weights left on the floor, edges of scenic trucks that stuck out – or just got my sandals caught either side of cables. This never did much for my suave woman-of-the-world image!

I inevitably made several false exits out of the office as well. Back for my clipboard with all the information on it about that evening's show, then back for my handbag and then back again for my torch. At least there were no guns in the show, as that used to be an even more incongruous sight: women and men in evening dress with armfuls of loaded rifles (blanks, of course), ready to hand them over to the firing squad or Napoleon's army.

I dumped my armful of working life in the prompt corner and surrendered to the task of speaking to Rudolf about the party. I phoned the stage door and, yes, he was in.

The dressing-room door was shut. I hovered for a while by the large, rather unflattering mirror that was hung just by the swing doors for 'artistes' to have a last-minute check. It brought back memories of the days when *Peter Pan* was staged at the Coliseum, just for matinées, whilst operas were performed at night-time. I remembered coming through the pass doors to find Dave Allen standing there in his Captain Hook regalia and being asked by him to help him with his hook and cuffs. This time all I saw was a tall, curvy-figured stage manager with a not-so-wonderful English-rose red nose: all that fine weather and sun brought the freckles out to play all over my face.

I knocked and went into the dressing-room. A smiling megastar awaited me. He, too, had had a good day. The sun did this to everyone in London we decided. His new dresser was fussing around him incessantly while we talked and was even irritating me. I told Rudolf about the party and he just stood there and listened, the mood changed within a nanosecond. Whether it was from irritation about being reminded of responsibilities and chores he would rather not do, I don't know. He stared at me through the mirror, nostrils flared, hands on hips, tights with their large white elastic braces half on.

The dresser broke the moment by fiddling with Rudolf's braces, heaving one side up to his shoulder, not a move I would have made without being instructed. Rudolf stood erect, batted aside the dresser's attentions and told him to, 'Leave, wait outside, whatever, I don't care!' He then looked at me for a split second, considering, waiting for my reaction. I asked him whether he would be able to attend the reception and he shrugged with a downturned lip, which I assumed signalled assent. Rudolf then sat and went back to his make-up. The conversation was definitely over and there was to be no more social chitchat. I left, telling the dresser to go back into the room, and charged back to the security of my office. I had no idea which one of us had caused that mood change.

The evening performance at the Coliseum was about to start. This was a unique moment: with no Nureyev in the first piece, we could start on time, although this was a white-knuckle ride backstage. On these nights, our evenings also had the added 'what if?' factor. Was he coming to warm up before? Would he arrive during the show? After we had started? What if this was the first time he didn't show up, didn't perform?

That night he was in residence, warming up in the wings using a practice barre whilst the first ballet went on.

I watched the performance as usual and naturally looked up as one of the soloists, a ballerina, came off the stage. She was petite, gorgeous, bejewelled and swearing like a trouper.

'If that fucking conductor can't conduct that fucking piece how I fucking want it, I will really sort him out.'

Hands on hips, she was 5 ft 2 in. of be-tutued attitude. Exquisitely made up, delicately formed and seriously cheesed off, she duck-footed her way up the wings, tutu bouncing, muttering and cursing, before entering the stage again as everyone's dream of the perfect ballerina, to dance wonderfully and enchant the audience.

One evening on stage, the small in-set scenery for *Le Spectre de la Rose* was being checked. The lighting director was walking around the stage, talking into a radio microphone to convey his requests for stage lights to be brought up and down to the guys in the lighting box at the back of the stalls. The iron curtain was in and the audience were in so this was the only method of communication to re-set any lights and check them between ballets.

Some of the original costumes that dancers wear are very antiquated. Although Rudi had made a point of redesigning most of his costumes, with short jackets to emphasise his figure, this particular one was in the Diaghilev mode. I found it very, very hard not to smile when Rudi used to walk on to the stage for *Spectre* during the short interval. He appeared to be wearing a swimming cap with a bit of old vine wrapped round it on his head. He was telling me to make sure that the special lights on the window ramps for his entrance didn't look like 'raspberries'. Said with a heavy Russian accent it sounded hilarious.

We were not helped by our chief electrician that night being 'Fifi', a name earned over the years both for his overuse of pink and also his wonderful campness. Rudolf and Fifi were old hands at the raspberries game and a quick sharp exchange of views on the subject ensued. I was not sure what the choice was here. If you have to have that colour and it is covering an entrance ramp which allowed him to seemingly just appear at the window, there seemed little to discuss. But discuss it they did – though Fifi always rolled over and never stood up to Rudolf. He walked away and Rudolf won the game.

Once the debate was over, the ballerina placed herself in the armchair with her rose in her hand and we sent the conductor down to the pit.

This was a fast-moving night. *Spectre* was short and stunning to watch. The ballerina dreaming of the ghost of the rose, who appears to her, set to Berlioz's fabulous music.

The curtain came in. After brief curtain calls we were in another interval and set the stage for *L'Après-midi d'un Faune*, and upstage of the *Faune* cloth, *Petrouchka* was set. We had our own set of 'Babushka' dolls on stage, starting with the smallest set for *Spectre*, then *Faune*, then *Petrouchka*.

I adore Debussy, but find *Faune* an unsettling piece. I am never sure of the nymphs who enter and dance to the faun and his pan pipes.

There was another interval, then came the highlight for me,

Petrouchka. This was a delight, full of extras and children doing their part out in the 'snow', and, of course, Rudi's phenomenal performance as the puppet come to life. *Petrouchka* is a scary piece for the novice stage manager as the music, a continuous drum roll, just carries on when you are doing the scene changes. But the crew were on form, running off 30-ft tall flats and then lashing new ones together as I gave the green light to the conductor to say that we were ready – just in time.

We had full stage curtain calls at the end of this night, the curtain coming in and out many times. You learned to shout loudly at a young age at the Coliseum: 'Everyone forward'; 'Everyone back'; 'Conductor next, please'; 'Curtain coming in'. The props staff rushed on to the stage to page (hold) open the curtain and let the dancers through for their calls. Rudolf asked me to wait whilst he dried off before his call. The calls lasted for about 20 minutes and even then everyone wanted more. There were piles of flowers on the stage and the horrible streak of body make-up along the front of the Coliseum house curtain was getting worse as the ballet season continued.

That night Rudolf was cross about the lighting, the music, the crowds in the wings – and he fired questions at me. 'Who were all those people?' – mostly his friends. 'The music was too fast here' and 'too slow here', 'lighting dreadful'. He eventually tailed off by telling me, 'You mustn't let all those people watch.' I couldn't help but laugh at this last barked remark and he sniffed loudly.

'So, it wasn't a good show?' I asked him.

'Not good, not bad. My foot is bad, I am getting too old. Maybe Old Galoshes should stick to dancing with Miss Piggy?' A hollow smile.

I noticed one of the actors or extras hovering, waiting for Nureyev. I thought, 'You'll be lucky', but in fact he had some photos for me. They were rather sweet of Rudi and me talking during curtain calls. He wondered if I would like them. I would have loved them, so why on earth did I say rather offhandedly, in fact rather grandly, 'Lovely, but no thanks.' What I would give to have those now. How stupid I was to have refused them and what a wonderful memento they would have made.

I was at the theatre long after the audience had left because, as usual, I had the show report to type out and distribute. Then I got changed and wandered through the hordes of visitors waiting outside the number-one dressing-room. I waved as I went by and called out, 'See you tomorrow.' This was followed by a shout, 'What time tomorrow, Caroline?' from the room. I stopped to tell him and then carved my way through the seemingly endless crowds.

Out on Bedfordbury was the usual mob of fans. Roger Myers, in Australia, used to hate driving Rudolf back to the hotel. 'I was scared that we would run someone over. There were hundreds of people all pushing against the car, trying to see Rudi. I hated that part of the evening. It was frightening.'

The next night was full of highlights. During the first interval I spotted Rudolf being carried off hanging on to his rehearsal barre! It was very funny.

Geoff, assisted by George, one of the other prop staff, was telling Rudi: 'Come on, Rudi, enough practice, you should know it by now and I want to get back to my pint, stop practising.' When Rudolf didn't stop, the two staff just picked up the barre with him hanging on to it. Rudolf feigned annoyance and just moved along with the guys until they all stopped and then he started at the barre again.

In the second interval, Al, the head flyman, came up to me in hysterics. There were tears pouring down his face. He was incapable of speaking. He was mopping his eyes with tissues, gasping and coughing. Well, it must have been good, whatever it was.

He gradually gasped out the story.

'You know where Rudi always leaves his clogs and that awful sweaty pile of tissues?'

'Yes, go on.'

'Well, Johnny P. [one of the crew] nailed down Rudi's clogs to the floor. Rudi came off, put his feet into the clogs and, of course, found that he couldn't move. He was pretending to be really angry but you could tell he thought it was funny.'

I should have been horrified as it could have had the most awful consequences for the star, but it was very funny.

'His clogs? No, that's too funny,' laughed Violette Verdy when I told her the story.

Ted Murphy, then one of the master carpenters at the Coliseum recalled, 'You know, Rudi really got on well with all the guys at the Coliseum. These were his mates just mucking around and Rudi knew that. They had all known Rudi for years. Geoff came over with Margot Fonteyn and Australian Ballet, and some of them had been on numerous tours with London Festival Ballet and all the others.' In the midst of tension and the search for perfection there was sometimes time for fun as well.

And once the mood was with everyone, of course, there was another joke that night. This time it was Harry L.'s turn. He was standing by with the rest of the crew on the prompt side, stage left. They were there to strike the scenery at the end of *Petrouchka* for the curtain calls, as we weren't able to page the tabs with the scenery in place.

Harry dropped his trousers and mooned for Rudi at precisely the right moment for Rudi to get the full impact as he fell through the paper flat. Of course, he had an audience of as many of the crew as could fit in down the prompt side.

When Rudi came off, Harry asked him, 'How did you like that?'

Rudolf replied, 'All I could see was a lot of piles,' and went on to do the curtain calls.

That was a good happy night followed immediately by a bad one.

This was the first time I saw a 'bad' performance by Rudolf, at least one that I could spot. Rudolf seemed lumpy, it was all a huge effort, and it was not good. I wondered how he was going to react. The curtain call at the end of *Spectre* was brief, professional and no comment was made.

Faune had gone well and in the mêlée of *Petrouchka*, where the sight lines were limited, I didn't get a chance to see what was really happening. No one made any comment so I assumed all was well.

During one of the solo calls that night, as he came back through the tabs, Rudolf talked to me about an injustice that he found intolerable. The conductor had allegedly been left off an invitation list for an after-show party, and this had really upset Rudolf. He was talking about the rudeness of people and said if there was a cost factor then just 'tell me' and he would pay for it. It is difficult to catch up on a conversation like this if you don't have all the facts and I, quite frankly, had no clue what to do. I, too, liked the conductor, but it really had got under Rudolf's skin that he had been omitted and to Rudolf's mind deliberately so. This outrage and his dancing had contributed to what appeared to be a bad night.

He was ranting and shouting, and was incredibly abusive about the promoter. Although he had made similar comments before, he had never been so pointedly anti-Semitic. I tried to calm him down but he would have none of it. Rudolf waved his hand; he had had enough. He walked away alone, grabbed a towel from the scenic brace and left in silence.

The next day our routine was disturbed by a rehearsal for a cast change and brought an unexpected moment of warmth.

I was asked to take the curtain out and I sauntered out onto the stage to ask the conductor what he would like, where he wanted to go from, which act, scene or what 'bits' he wanted to do with the orchestra. When I walked out, I was surprised to see the whole of the dress circle filled with 'Friends' (of the theatre). I walked out onto the forestage and stared at hundreds of people, who instinctively went silent in case I was about to say anything interesting. You always get a good atmosphere on days such as these, as audiences love to see 'mistakes' or re-runs, although we always tried to ensure that this never ever happened.

Even though I hadn't been told about them, I still went out onto the stage to speak to the conductor. It always seemed so remote and inhuman to shout out all the questions invisibly. The rehearsal went smoothly and we brought the curtain in at the end. I was asked to get some crew to set barres on the stage in a square, and they needed the piano on stage as well. I was intrigued.

Through the pass door came a crocodile of anxious mums, with attendant five- and six-year-olds grasping their mothers' hands for all their worth. They were invited onto the stage and they slotted in between the dancers, their fingertips barely reaching the barres and their furiously concentrating faces creased and frowning. They wore long white socks in ballet slippers and their school uniforms. It was a joy to see. I thought of all the children going to dance classes around the world, going through their paces in all the draughty school and church halls. What would they have given to stand on the Coliseum stage with real dancers?

The mums were lined up, anxious, proud and ready to move to help at any moment. As the pianist went through their almost mechanical routine, Rudolf walked onto the stage. He had changed into his usual practice clothes: all-in-one knitted jumpsuit and, of course, a knitted hat.

Standing with his hands on his hips he watched everyone, stars and children alike. He moved round some of the dancers to talk to them, and helped them. Then he assessed the children.

He carefully took one small foot after another, gently pointing the toe and then placing the leg back in first position again. It was done with such incredible care, yet seriously and with encouragement. I wonder if any of those wide-eyed prospective dancers remember this moment.

There was murmured laughter, cooing and smiles. It was a really precious moment for everyone, including me.

I went to see him after this rehearsal. He had a lightness about him and was very relaxed. I said how lovely it had been to see the little ones trying to reach the barre. It seemed to have been a very special moment for him, too.

It was the next evening and I had paused by his room. We got onto his favourite topic of conversation, architecture and theatres, and I asked him, 'Did you know that they once had a bridge between the two huge gilded lions [at the top on either side of the proscenium arch] that you could walk across?'

'Yes, I have seen photos,' he replied.

'The Coliseum chandeliers are so high up that you cannot really appreciate how big they are. I think I have only ever seen them lowered once, in the early '70s,' I said.

Rudolf talked of the chandeliers in the Russian theatres, in Denmark, in France, everywhere he had danced. We talked about the Kirov theatre, with its blue and gold auditorium, the beautiful chandeliers and the fact that the Coliseum was bigger and held a larger audience. Rudolf told me about the segregation at the Kirov, how the male dancers were on one side of the stage, and the women on the other. I was sure that I remembered touring to provincial theatres in England where the chorus rooms were split into male and female to help dressers and for the showers, but not in London.

I asked him where his favourite theatre was and I was surprised that he did not bat me away. Instead, out came a long list divided between people, cities and the ballets performed there. I asked him whether the first Russian theatre he danced in was special for him. He didn't answer, but looked at me. One question too many, or too close to home? I was still learning what I could ask and when. It was difficult being selective for a Russian, having spent fun moments listening and laughing with the film star Sir Alan Bates about his day with no no-go areas.

I felt I was a long way from getting close to this star, but I persevered. Continuing on the same theme, I asked Rudolf whether he had seen Fellini's movie *Casanova* with Donald Sutherland. One image in particular had stayed with me from this film and, like two over-anxious school kids trying to outdo one another, we both say at the same time, 'the scene with the chandeliers being lowered!'

Huge chandeliers, all alight with hundreds of candles, were lowered to the ground to the sound of squeaking chains. As they reached the polished wooden floor, a group of men walked up to them. There was a pair of servants to each chandelier. The scene was very evocative, no music, just chains and footsteps and the massive visual impact of these vast, spectacular chandeliers being lowered in.

The men then worked in pairs, one spun each chandelier, whilst the other fanned out the flames with a large unwieldy wooden paddle, until all the candles were out.This scene made a huge impact on me at the time. It was incredibly atmospheric.

I said to Rudolf that I thought I would have been one of the 'fanners' in a past life: woken up at 3 a.m., dragged from my shelf in a cupboard somewhere to perform this task. Rudolf laughed and said that he was up in the roof working the chains, unseen, receiving no thanks.

Somehow, Mr Nureyev, I don't think so.

CHAPTER FIVE

Let's Go Hunting

I watched as the solitary figure moved in and out of the pools of orange sodium lighting. This was a novel lighting effect and, for a moment, this particular stage belonged to him, a flamboyant alley cat turned a mandatory grey.

He gradually made his way up Whitworth Street in Manchester for a night of hunting.

Slight and elegant, but with that giveaway splayed-feet walk, he slowly disappeared towards the horizon, leaving behind the domed magnificence of the Prudential Insurance building. He was dwarfed by the huge red-brick Victorian buildings with pavement-level leaded lights, the glass bricks inset into the pavement to give the workers some daylight in the huge basements where the machine age rumbled and ruled the lives of the workers in nineteenth-century Manchester.

He became smaller and smaller and then was gone.

I turned away from the theatre and headed back to my hotel, thinking that he had looked surprisingly vulnerable. I tried not to imagine the worst that could happen to him. He was one of the most famous people in the world, someone who made headline news just for smiling, let alone what he was probably hoping to do that night. There was no need to fuss whilst he hit the more notorious areas of this northern city, I told myself; he had done this many times before all around the world and must know what he was doing.

In 1983, I had an unexpected phone call from Victor Hochhauser

Ltd. Although I was working on the London season as well, Sander Gorlinsky, Rudolf's manager, wanted someone to 'watch over everything'. So, I went up to Manchester to stay with Boston Ballet and see them safely down to London for the season.

Manchester has been renowned for its hedonism since its Victorian days. Home to a vibrant punk scene in the late '70s, bars, pubs and entertainment earned the city the title of 'Madchester' in the late '80s.

The poverty of the Victorian industrial era, with its sweatshops and sharply defined class lines, created a need to find relaxation through cheaper forms of entertainment. This was the environment that encouraged Engels to wander off the path of pure idealism and into the city's drinking dens, in between penning thoughts to Karl Marx.

Mancunian nightlife also created a unique ritual in the nineteenth and early twentieth century called 'the Monkey Run', a British version of the way Mediterranean families and young men walked out in the evening in towns and cities. Both sexes dressed up in their best or most original clothes for the run. According to Dave Haslam's book *Manchester, England*, these 'parades' were so important that if your best suit was in the pawnbrokers then you missed the monkeying until you could pay to 'pop' it again, to get it back. You never went out not looking the part on the Monkey Run.

Sex was seemingly on offer everywhere, with wonderful turns of phrase from working ladies, who would woo men by asking if they could be introduced to 'Fagin'.

In this historic setting, I had watched Nureyev set off to 'conquer', dressed for his own version of the Monkey Run.

I asked Bill Akers and Roger Myers if they had ever watched Rudi set out for one of these nightly expeditions.

'Roger and I used to eat at the Charles Noir, in Nice. It was a small restaurant and one that basically we could afford,' remembered Bill. 'This was about 1964. It was our first time abroad and we had no money. The maître d' used to walk around the restaurant on his toes. He was a complete *Cages aux folles* all to himself. He was camp, entertaining and very funny.

'We were eating our meal one night when Rudi came in. He was dressed in the smallest pair of white shorts, very like the ones in that lovely photo of Robert and Rudi on Rhodes, and a tight white singlet showing off the body beautiful. Which, of course, it was: very, very beautiful.

'We had no idea why he had chosen this particular restaurant at all but he sat down and joined us for a few drinks and then said to Roger and me, "Let's go downstairs to the *cave*." We did not know what this was, but we followed him downstairs anyway.

'He caused an incredible stir wherever he went. You know that wonderful way the French have of pronouncing his name and they spell it differently as well, "Noureïev"? Well, this mutter used to go round the room wherever he was, "Noureïev, Noureïev", as every part of the room looked up and noticed him.

'We were amazed. The *cave* turned out to be a bar, but only for men. It was just full of men drinking and talking, nothing else. This was a completely new world to us. Australia in the 1960s was very much a British colony from a different era. Whilst England was swinging in the '60s we were stuck somewhere in 1955. Gay bars, even swearing and discussing sex, were unheard of.

'We stayed drinking in the *cave* for a while and that is when he said, "Let's go hunting."

'We piled into his tiny sports car and headed out around the bars. He was a nightmare of a driver and this car could only really take two people, though there were the three of us squashed in. We stopped at the first bar and went into it. The murmurs and looks of recognition as Rudi entered were extraordinary, "Noureïev!" Roger and I ordered the drinks whilst Rudi did a stately circuit of the whole bar, hands in his shorts pockets, knowing how wonderful he looked. All these bars were elliptical in shape and he would come back to us after his circuit of the entire bar, finish his drink and say: "No good." And off we went again.

'We got back into the car and drove on to the next likely-looking bar. We went to bar after bar all night and he went through the same process in each one. All the while we were getting more and more merry. Roger and I were getting worried about leaving Rudi and having him drive back on his own to his house. The thought of him driving when he was in that state and on those cliff roads did not bear thinking about. Roger and I had had enough really and after the next "no good", we suggested that we went back to our hotel and he could stay there. Of course, we were being rather naive as he probably hoped that a *ménage à trois* was on the cards – he had always had a soft spot for Roger. He could not have been more wrong.

'We went up to my room and Rudi immediately spotted a jewellery box of mine at the end of the room. He went over to it and said, "Pig, you have more jewellery than me!" Well, we were all really very relaxed with the drink by now, and whilst Rudi was up the other end of the room, Roger and I turned and ran. We locked Rudi into my room. Looking back at this, it was not our best move.

'When we got up the next morning, we had breakfast and went to the theatre. When we arrived, everyone was going mad in the rehearsal room, "Where's Rudi? No one's seen Rudi." Then, with utter horror, we remembered. Joan Thring was working on publicity for the tour and I told her that Rudi was in my room. To which she replied with huge undertones, "Oh, yes?"

'I had to explain that there was no "oh, yes" about it so I told her the whole story. "My God," she said, "he will demolish that room." We dashed back to the hotel to unlock the room, only to find Rudi still there and sound asleep.

'Needless to say we were not that popular for the rest of the tour.'

Bill then recalls, 'Rudi spent hours lusting after one of our young dancers, a really good-looking young man. Day after day he would try to chat up this guy and he really was not interested. Rudi even asked me if I would go and fix it for him. I pretended that I was shocked, as it was all in good fun, and I said that I did not do that sort of thing. "Do it yourself, you ask him."

'Well, he drove us all mad, and finally in mock desperation I went up to the young guy and said, "Look, will you do us all a favour and get Rudi off our backs? It will not hurt for long." It was a joke and we were all having a bit of fun. The young guy replied with a huge, "Urgh. No thanks, I do not like the smell of him." It was all a joke.

'But a few weeks later, the pressure stopped and we were all left wondering if he had "done the right thing". It was very funny, you know, "for Queen and country". We never found out what had happened but it was all done in good humour.'

'There are so very many stories,' Violette Verdy recalls. 'Peter

Martins used to say that all Rudi needed after a performance was a steak and a boy. One time we were all snorkelling in Miami and Rudolf got so very sunburned. You should have seen him. He was in just a G-string and we had to cover him with creams to help him. Oh, it was so bad we were all laughing at how bad it was. Maybe he had to take a night off that night. A steak, yes, but no boy!

'He even made a pass at my partner at the time, Mahôt [Jean-Pierre de la Querantomnias]. It was hysterical. He was talking to Rudolf and Rudolf told him to follow him into the bathroom. And, of course, Rudi was only wearing a towel and he let it drop to the ground. I was in the other room, and Mahôt came back to tell me that he had "never seen anything so big". Mahôt told Rudi that it really wasn't for him and Rudolf just said that if he changed his mind to let him know. It was so funny.

'But, you know, Rudolf even made a pass at Anton Dolin, the former Ballets Russes star. He was driven by this engine about all of this. He never stopped.'

'Then, of course, there were all the nightclubs that we went to,' Bill Akers recollects. 'There was a wonderful moment one time when we all went out dancing and, of course, Rudi was the focus of everyone's attention. We were all doing the twist, except that he could not do it. He looked like a classical ballet dancer trying to be beautiful while doing this dance, it was hysterical. He looked at me and said "Pig. You do it better than me." He really did do it so badly.'

Manchester in 1983 did not quite compare to Nice in 1964. Later we were to learn that 1983 was when Rudi started to have night sweats and to experience the symptoms of Aids. There was no test for Aids at this time, so it was not diagnosed until 1985. He was still out playing and having unprotected sex. His physician, Doctor Michel Canesi, was to report later that he believed that he had been HIV positive from as early as 1977 or 1978.

Robert said that Rudolf adored Manchester because the theatre was so beautiful and the audiences liked him. I adored Manchester, too. I had been on tour there many times. First with English National Opera and then with various plays. Manchester is one of the major cities that touring shows visit, hopefully before moving on to

London. The major opera and ballet companies and other productions always wanted to go to most of these 'number ones', theatres in the more important cities or towns such as Bristol, Leeds, Newcastle, Brighton, Birmingham and Manchester, before heading for home or on to a successful West End run. Going to these cities and towns provided a chance for the productions to settle in, for any necessary changes to be made and to gather reviews. This was an expensive process, especially if it turned into one of the huge overseas tours that used to happen in the '70s and '80s. If you were lucky enough to join one of these, you could rattle off long lists of the cities that you had been paid to visit.

'I think we did Glasgow, Liverpool, London Covent Garden, Paris, Copenhagen, Berlin, back to London at the New Victoria, Paris again – this time the Palais des Sports – then Hawaii. All with Rudolf and Margot,' recalls Bill Akers. They don't do tours like that any more, except for rock or pop groups, of course.

For me, the warmth and humour of the northern theatres and the towns and cities was wonderful. I could not get over people smiling and speaking to me when I walked into a shop or just down the street. In London, that just did not happen. There was also the lure of the art galleries and museums, the architecture of these proud northern towns and the wonderful countryside surrounding the cities.

I loved the sheer scale of some of the buildings. There were a great many Victorian red-brick 'statements' with huge high windows and imposing turrets, arches and cupolas meeting the sky.

On one tour with ENO, we arrived at Manchester to find ourselves following the Danny La Rue show. There was and always is such a wide selection of shows at these huge touring houses.

I never met Danny La Rue, but Bill Akers did, while he was with Rudolf and Margot.

'We took Margot and Rudi out one night to see Danny La Rue at his club in London. He used to do this take-off of the pas de deux from *Swan Lake* with Ronnie Corbett. Ronnie played Rudi. Margot had lent one of her costumes to them so that they could copy it. It was really a very funny act, but Rudi thought that they were aping him unkindly, when it was all just a joke and a bit of fun and part of their routine act. He thought that they were doing it especially because he was in that night,' recalls Bill Akers.

During our conversations, I told Bill about Manchester and we spoke about the anonymity which must have been a huge attraction, no fans and no photographers. Bill remembered, 'You know when we were in Nice and Rudi was being fêted everywhere we went? He was just so famous. Everything was there for him whenever he wanted it. I think that it must have been to him like the lure of fruitcake for someone who has never ever seen or eaten fruitcake before in their life. All of a sudden, they discover that they can have it, all of it, when and wherever they want. I think that is what happened to Rudi.' In Manchester, as Bill said, 'He was just another person, albeit a beautiful one, out looking for fun, with no obligation, no commitment. But out hunting or cruising there was no one to say "no" to him. He could have as much "fruitcake" as he wanted.'

I asked Robert about Rudolf's desire for solitude when he went out.

'He definitely liked being alone a lot, cruising or whatever else. I'm surprised they let him get away with that.'

'They' being the press?

'Yes.' Well, we all knew about it, yet the press and any potential kiss-and-tells never made an issue of it. He was very lucky when you consider the much-publicised more recent excursions into the night of stars like George Michael and Hugh Grant. Perhaps the press considered it more newsworthy in the '90s. Also, back in Manchester in 1983, we had yet to be stunned by the death of Rock Hudson in 1985, the first household name to tell the world that he had been suffering from Aids.

When the Nureyev circus came to town, it was a bright, hot summer's day in Manchester. Four coaches pulled up outside the hotel and a large group of tired dancers staggered out to tell a major tale of woe. They had no suitcases, no costumes, no shoes, nothing. They had come from Rome via London to Manchester and they had watched their suitcases stay firmly on the tarmac as they took off.

As I listened, I wondered how we were going to manage if the cases really were lost and did not make the show. Then, suddenly,

Robert Tracy was there on the pavement, smiling, dressed in a white T-shirt and cool khaki trousers with a bag slung over his shoulder. We were both very pleased to see each other. Robert was there as a member of Boston Ballet and was to dance in their premiere of *Don Quixote*. It was a very important event.

We negotiated toothbrushes, soap and basic stuff for the dancers. But there was a problem to solve: what should we do about costumes, specifically Rudolf's? Calls were made to the other ballet companies in the UK, just in case the luggage did not arrive. Despite the carefully controlled panic in the voice and the determined 'No, of course I am sure it is going to be fine,' that closed each conversation, we all knew there was no guarantee.

We bedded down for the night and hoped for the best. The scenery and lighting were all with us so we could at least start that part of the week safely. An air of optimism was essential, how else was all the hard work going to get done that would result in a great first night in Manchester? We eventually got the good news that the costumes were on their way. It had been a close call but the emergency plans were not needed after all.

During the lighting rehearsal, I discovered that all was not well between Rudolf and the company. There was a rumour of a punch-up between Rudi and a stagehand, and this seemed to be confirmed by a state of non-communication between some parts of the company and Nureyev. It turned out to be true but I never found out the whole story; naturally with a premiere to stage, everyone was keeping very quiet about it. It was a bizarre situation, which I did not fully appreciate until, Bob Scott, the theatre manager, asked me if Nureyev would come to a party after the first night hosted by the Friends of the Manchester Palace. I tried to look as if this would not be a problem and said of course I would ask.

Now, I have asked hundreds of people to come to these events around the UK and far lesser mortals than Nureyev have come back with a normally unpublishable reply. So, did I really think that Rudi would do this? Not a chance. I wondered if it was actually worth all the aggravation of asking him and putting myself in the firing line like this, but my instinct was to ask him because you just never knew.

These local events can be seen as tedious and avoidable by stars and performers, but they are essential to foster good relations between the theatre and the touring company and great for the people who join these clubs. To be a 'Friend' of a theatre gives people a wonderful opportunity to steal sneak previews and glimpses of what goes on backstage. They can also be invited to lectures and, of course, the occasional 'do'.

The number-one dressing-room was on the right-hand side, called 'opposite prompt' or OP. It was set down a few steps and was painted a rather lurid pink with a red carpet and a huge, ancient, deep crimson settee. Sitting on the right-hand side, putting on his make-up, was my challenge for the day.

I decided that a straight question might get me a straight reply, and so it did. 'Will you come to a small drinks party after the show for the Friends of the theatre, they would be thrilled if you would?'

'You pick me up and take me?'

'Yes, of course.'

'I will come.'

'Oh, great, thanks, they will be delighted.'

I was astounded that without hesitation he said yes. This was extraordinary.

The first hurdle was over. Getting him to turn up would be the next test.

The show went well and he was on good form. There was still an atmosphere, though. We talked during the intervals about the Frank Matcham theatres outside London, then Rudolf asked me if I had been to any of the new clubs around town. He wanted to know which were good and what was going on in the city. Of course, he knew that I would not have a clue. And I knew that he enjoyed asking me about things that I would have no idea about, nor would I have wanted to. It was part of his game, to learn as much as possible about you and then leave you to realise that you had learnt nothing about him during the whole process.

As I left, he reminded me to collect him after the show to go to this 'do'. He was the only person in the world to make the word 'do' sound exotic, more like 'Dooh'.

I spent the evening hovering and being in the way. I was asked questions about merchandising and programmes that I knew nothing about. I tried to make a break for freedom through the pass door just as Rudolf came over to me. He whined about the conductor and asked for his dresser, which at least gave me a task. The performance of *Don Quixote* was received well and the audience gave the company a taste of the length of the curtain calls they could expect in London.

I waited outside his dressing-room then knocked and entered down the steps into the pink boudoir. He was ready and said, 'Let's go to this party!' with a wry smile. I think he had a suspicion what it was going to be like.

On our way, he stopped to look at the auditorium. I quite liked the colour of this theatre; it was part of its charm. It was a rich, almost salmon, pink, with boards rather like hymn number boards on either side of the proscenium arch. These were a relic from the days of variety shows, when numbers were slotted into them to show the audience who was on next. We then arrived at the front-of-house bar where the reception was being held.

It was quite an entrance. I was sure by the looks on the faces of the good burghers of Manchester, their wives and the Friends that they had not really thought he would come. Neither had I. When I told Bill Akers this story all these years later, he couldn't believe it, 'He never did that sort of thing.' He obviously really did like being in Manchester.

Standing resplendent in his leather jacket, brown suede trousers and mandatory hat, Rudolf stood in the centre of the room, gratefully receiving a glass of white wine and taking a sausage roll whilst waiting to be approached by these favoured fans. He stayed and talked, smiled and listened, and surely gave everyone a moment to remember. Here, I thought, was a true professional doing his duty. I was so naive. It had not occurred to me that there could be another reason why he would welcome such a diversion that filled in a gap before he disappeared through the stage door. It ensured that he wouldn't be seen arriving too early. By arriving later, you could see who was there and assess the 'prey'.

I asked Robert about their cruising, but Robert remained firm, saying, 'If you want to learn about cruising, then read Joe Orton.'

This late-night habit had apparently started during Nureyev's time at the Kirov. After any performance, Rudi would need to go out and relax for hours, not necessarily doing anything other than winding down from the adrenalin high of a performance.

Robert and Rudolf would go out together but play separately, then return home together. I asked Robert what he thought about Rudi going out hunting when he was by this time obviously ill and it was so dangerous. Robert said that one night when Rudolf came back and reported having had unprotected sex with a hustler, Rudolf had actually wondered what he might have caught from the hustler. Robert silently wanted to shake Rudolf and say, 'Never mind him and what he has given to you, what have you given to him?'

I rather naively asked Robert why he had not said anything, 'Are you kidding? Come on, you know what he was like.' Rudolf was in denial for so long. Aids had not been diagnosed then in 1983 and though Rudolf had the symptoms, he did not yet link it to unprotected sex. Or maybe he did not want to. Robert, on the other hand, had read more and understood more and made more informed choices.

'I wanted Rudolf to see my spiritual adviser, my guru,' recalls Violette Verdy. 'Rudolf was very spiritual and I thought this would be a wonderful opportunity for him.'

'He said that he thought that my guru would tell him to stop having sex. That was his major concern. I told him it would probably be the reverse, but he would have more of an understanding and get more enjoyment from the sex.

'He then started to make a joke about it. It was his way of ignoring it and in a way changing the subject. He was unbelievable the way he could make very sophisticated jokes in so many languages. So he used to ask me, "Was there a *Who's Who* for gurus?" over and over. He loved the sound of the words. It was so funny.'

The drug culture at the time and the partying would have been part of their lives, surely, but Robert says that this was his culture not Rudolf's.

'It was a big deal for Rudolf to even take an aspirin.' This cannot have been easy towards the end. I remembered reading that his doctor had found nearly full bottles of the prescribed medication that Rudolf was meant to have taken.

Robert told me, 'I remember Rudolf saying, "Well, if they have cured syphilis they will cure this." But that was the homosexuals' nemesis. Antibiotics. We believed they would cure everything, and Rudolf thought so too at the time – before he knew that it was Aids – that penicillin would clear it up in a couple of days.'

Robert believes that Rudolf, like many gay men, was poisoned by the drug AZT, which he insisted he needed. There is a famous article 'Petrouchka was poisoned', about Nureyev, on the Internet, which goes into great detail, questioning the validity of AZT, the lack of clinical trials and the 'poisonous side-effects'. 'But he still lived for ten years more which was incredible,' said Robert.

Back in Manchester, after Rudolf's night of prowling, there was a press call the next morning to publicise the London season. This was unusual as neither Rudolf nor the companies were usually available in the UK prior to the season. As this was Nureyev, it was bound to attract a lot of attention and was a chance for regional reporters to get close to the star.

I do not have a great record with press calls in Manchester. Keeping the press at bay for more than two hours on another occasion, with another star, not Rudolf, was one of my least favourite experiences. The thought of this press call filled me with dread as it was early and there was no guarantee that he would show up.

I waited outside the front of the theatre with a growing number of photographers, facing up the street towards the hotels. There was an air of resigned pessimism. They kept looking at me every few minutes to see if I was going to reveal whether or not he was going to arrive. I tried to keep a professional fixed smile and a look of optimism on my face. I was apprehensive but I should have remembered that he had not let me down so far. In fact, he did not let me down ever.

On the dot of eleven, a hand touched my shoulder: it was Rudi. He had come round the side of the theatre from where I had watched him disappear the night before. He stood beside me waiting for the photographers to turn round and see him. I assumed that he had not been back to the hotel after his night checking out the hidden corners and delights of Manchester.

Rudolf smiled at me and was enjoying this moment looking at the backs of the press. He was revelling in their wrong-footedness, all of them facing the wrong way. It was his moment of theatrical triumph and surprise.

I could not bear it any longer and said loudly to the sea of backs, 'Ladies and gentlemen.' They turned and Rudi stood with his arms stretched out saying, 'So?' He loved it and posed for the photographers outside the rather stark cream and red tiles of the theatre front.

The reporter from the *Express* came over to me and said, 'I expected it to be like last time you were here, when the other one didn't show up for hours and you told us some garbage about him being on the phone to the US.' They do have very long memories.

Inside the theatre, this motley procession headed by Rudi, the press officer and myself clambered up the staircase, Rudolf trying to lead the way. But we had gone up the wrong staircase, and tried in vain to open the locked glass door to the bar where we could see the cameras were already set up. Rudolf was seriously unimpressed and suddenly demanding.

The London promoter chaired the meeting, with Rudolf on his left facing a barrage of cameras and notepads. Questions flew round about Manchester, the ballets, the company, what he had been doing, was he well, how was he dancing – dangerous ground – and finally someone asked, 'When are you going back to Russia?' Before Rudi could reply, the promoter diplomatically stepped in and the session was over. With Rudolf's mother so ill back in Russia it was a long-term wish of his to be allowed to return to see her. His wish was eventually granted in 1987.

I think we were all aware of his mother being ill, but that was the first time I had heard any public mention of his need to get back to Russia, although I am sure it had been mentioned in the press. There was always so much about Rudolf in the press.

When the Bolshoi came over in the '70s, the technical director of the Bolshoi gave Ted Murphy and other members of the crew at the Coliseum lots of pin badges from the ballet company, which Ted kept.

One night, nearly ten years later, during one of the Nureyev Festival seasons in the '80s, Ted wore some of the badges that had been given to him during the visit of the Bolshoi. Ted had pinned them on his T-shirt. 'I just wore them for the fun of it. They were nice things to have, good mementos of nice people and good times. Rudi came off the stage and saw these badges. He started ripping them off my shirt and stamping on them. He was screaming at me, "How can you wear these in front of me? My mother is dying and they won't let me see her and you are wearing these?"

'He was stamping them into the ground, he was so angry.

'I was shocked. I wouldn't have worn them if I'd known. I was trying to calm him and make it up with him. I said, "Rudi, I'm sorry, mate. I hadn't realised."' Ted says again today that he was so sorry he had done it as he had no idea about Rudi's mother, nor that it would upset him so much.

'It didn't occur to me. I didn't mean to hurt him.'

In that summer of 1983, we moved on to London, where the crew had to remember how to get to grips with American English with the crew from Boston Ballet. The usual question cropped up: how can we not speak the same language when we speak the same language? The crew got a lesson, too, in how efficiently the US team ran certain aspects of the technical side. They had crystal-clear, idiot-proof lists of what happened when and who was to do it. There were bags hanging behind scenery with pre-selected colour gels for the lanterns, all ready for the scene changes.

They struggled to get past the first communication problem of when is a bay (the space between two masking flats into the wings) not a bay, but an 'in' or an 'out'. Then they started to talk about 'killing' things and 'dead' things, which led to a discussion on the morbid vocabulary of the stage. We 'kill' lights when we do not need them; we talk of a prop or an item being 'dead' and no longer wanted or needed. To add confusion we set 'deads', levels or heights, on cloths, scenery or anything that is to be flown. I wondered if this vocabulary comes from the out-of-work sailors who used to work in the theatres – the traditional theatre crew in London from as far back as the sixteenth century. These were great conversations, often continued in the pub later on.

The atmosphere from Manchester followed us down to London. I felt as though I was standing to attention all the time. I felt on parade, ready for inspection with a centre parting, clean fingernails, shiny shoes and aching cheekbones from smiling all day. After all, this was the London premiere of *Don Quixote* for Boston Ballet, and very important for any ballet company.

The repertoire also included *Swan Lake* and although I had watched *Swan Lake* from the audience many times, I do not think you ever forget the first time you watch it from the wings and really see what is going on. This was my first time in 1983. I started to watch the different interpretations of the ballerinas and see the different ways in which Rudolf would handle them. I could also see that sometimes it was a huge effort, a grunt, to lift them. He would then stand back as they landed. There was not a lot of gallantry involved at times.

Everyone had spoken about Nureyev being panther-like, animal-like. Violette said that when he became a swan, he was both male and female. Now I finally had my chance to see him act, perform and 'become' a swan in order to love a swan.

Watching him in the final act made me gasp. He was so involved in the music and who he was; he ran, desperate to find Odile. I was standing stage right and I felt that he was going to just keep on running with that splendid fire in his eyes unless he met Odile at exactly the right moment. It was breathtaking.

In such contrast to the extraordinary beauty of the dances is the undertow of irreverence that pervades the theatre. I was transfixed by my first *Lac* (*Swan Lake*). But many of the crew called it 'Duck Pond'. *Giselle* became 'Gissethly', in a sudden burst of Welsh. And though I am just fascinated by the music, I am not sure Pyotr Ilyich Tchaikovsky envisaged a group of us singing along to the main theme in Act 2 of *Swan Lake*,with the words 'two lovely brown eyes' from the wings. It became a nightly routine and a good moment of laughter for all of us.

The set pieces were wonderful to watch and eventually I wheeled in my partner and a friend of his after they both muttered 'just a lot of poofs in tights' once too often. I thought that it was time for them to see the expertise and exertion for themselves. They were completely cured of their misinformed stereotypical prejudice as they watched the energy and artistry of the dancers. It also prompted a lot of talk, but only talk, of jogging and gym membership being renewed. If I remember correctly, a bull-worker, or chest expander, was even resurrected from its pride of place in an under-stair cupboard for at least a day.

There is a great finale to Act 2 in *Swan Lake,* where the female corps de ballet is on stage and they are joined by the soloists. The audience sees delicate beauty and hears only the music. But the noise under the stage at the Coliseum was incredible. I did not need to warn the crew that we were coming to an interval. The cry went up: 'Here they go', and it took just seconds for the entire crew – stage crew, props staff, wardrobe staff, wigs department, dressers and electricians – to make it on to the stage, ready for the interval and the scene change. It was finely timed.

During the run of the '83 season, when there were not any rehearsals on stage, our days started quite late, at about four or five in the afternoon. I used to like just sitting watching the class on stage. Everyone learning together and working together. No stars, just dancers.

We changed ballet companies again midway through the Nureyev Festival. Ballet Théâtre Français de Nancy was back for their second visit in my experience. It was a welcome return for the 'Homage de Diaghilev' programme. We were back in the world of actors and *Petrouchka* and no delays at the start because, again, we started with *Boutique Fantasque,* without Rudolf.

One night, when we should have been starting *Spectre* as the interval ended, we appeared to have a technical problem. Some pieces of *Petrouchka* scenery had hit the lighting ladders and the electricians were concerned that during the change from *Faune* to *Petrouchka* they would not have time to re-focus. So it made sense to correct this at that moment.

I phoned the front-of-house manager and explained that we would start late. He laughed, as he was about to give me clearance. Murphy's Law was working well that night, we both agreed. Rudolf was marking through, doing his own rough rehearsal of some of the ballet and had seen what the problem was. He was not bothered by the delay, as he wanted the lighting to be perfect. It also gave him more time to practise, and the audience was waiting patiently.

One of the directors of the visiting company came bustling through the pass door and confronted me about why we had not started. I laughed, considering what usually happened to us with our late starts. I was just about to explain that we had a problem when Rudolf stopped, looked straight at them and barked, 'Caroline is not ready. When Caroline is ready, we start.' Not a word more was said. The director beat a hasty retreat through the pass door.

I appeared to have crossed some threshold and from that moment on, I felt accepted. I was a non-threatening female who just wanted to get the show right.

A promoter had remarked to me that although Rudi was 'still very difficult', he would do anything I wanted. I would have done anything he wanted. Our professional relationship was one based on mutual respect and he and I never had a big falling out. He never swore at me, threw anything at me, but then I had also had the feeling that it was more than my life was worth to risk provoking him. It was a fine line, as when people failed to stand up to him, he made their life so difficult. He needed to know that you were not going to just let him get away with anything. Our spats were short, sharp and gone. Finished.

A rather novel masseur or dresser accompanied Rudolf this time. He was built like a weightlifter and Taiwanese, I think. He spoke no English, just gave a broad smile. A colleague and I mused that this one definitely was not employed for his conversation skills.

One night we nearly had a true disaster. It was Adam Harrison, a stage manager helping me on this season, who reminded me of the terrifying incident. 'Rudolf came off the stage and into the wings. His masseur handed a towel to him and Rudi hissed "water". The masseur turned round to the nearest table, picked up the bottle on it and extended it to Rudi. The performance was in full swing during all this. One of the crew instantly snatched the bottle away.

'It was white spirit, not water at all. In a plastic bottle looking like a bottle of mineral water, it had been mistaken in the semi-darkness,' remembered Adam.

White spirit was kept in readiness to quickly clean ballet shoes that had an excess of rosin on them. An icy chill goes through me whenever I remember this moment, as the consequences could have been awful. Luckily, Rudolf was just irritated at the delay in getting water and did not realise the danger he had been in.

Adam went on: 'Apart from that moment, what I remember most about this season was the sense of warmth and humour amongst everyone.'

Later that evening, we had some light relief. Alan, the head flyman, came onto the stage during an interval. He was slight, very good looking and an ex-ballet dancer. Dressed all in white, with tight jeans, he was difficult to miss; he looked very good and he knew it. Alan enjoyed challenging Rudi and Rudi always rose to it.

The whole company were on stage ready for the curtain up, which we rather irreverently called 'kick-off', as if we were at a football match. Alan stopped centre stage, prepared, put his right arm out, sucked in his cheeks, pursed his lips and did an admirable impersonation of Rudi. The cast looked on in stunned silence.

Rudolf took a look at Alan's proffered arm and managed to suck in his cheeks even more than Alan. He crossed to the centre of the stage and took Alan's hand. Without even a pause, they both performed a rough and ready version of the pas de deux from *Don Quixote*, with Alan as Basilio and Rudolf as Kitri, ending in a grand 'fishtail' swoop. There was applause and laughter from the cast. It was a wonderful moment and tremendous fun. Rudolf and Alan fell about laughing. Neither was thinking about what might have happened if Alan had dropped Rudi. Alan disappeared up to his eyrie back in the flys and Rudolf prepared for a 'serious' performance.

The rest of that week with Nureyev was fun and uneventful until we hit the first matinée. As usual, the night before, Rudi checked the time of the performance. At that point there didn't seem to be a problem, but on the afternoon of the matinée, Rudolf came down to the prompt corner. Fully clothed and looking determined, this did not bode well.

'Caroline, I cannot go on this afternoon. You will have to tell them.'

'You are joking?' I did not mean that exactly, I was just surprised.

This was Rudolf 'Never Off', going off! 'Are you all right? What is the problem?'

'I am tired and my ankle is bad.' I walked with him back to his dressing-room; I didn't quite believe that this was happening. He was incredibly quiet with his head hung low, looking at the floor. He looked deflated and depressed. I asked him about how he was going to get home and he said he would find his driver. 'What time is the performance tonight? I will go home and rest and come back for tonight.' So he was not joking, this was serious.

I had not believed this was ever going to happen.

The emergency plan swung into action, and the directors of the visiting ballet company were informed. It was their star's lucky day as he had the chance to perform. The management of the theatre had to be told, as over 2,000 people were not going to be that thrilled and one particular member of the audience was not going to be at all happy.

The house manager came round and we all took a deep breath. This was not going to be a fun announcement to make. It was almost unprecedented. It was one of those moments where Dutch courage and a cry of 'Don't shoot the messenger' were essential.

Even with notices around the foyer and all over the building there would be hundreds who would not have read them. The prop staff, myself and the house manager, a little group of Christians, gathered behind the curtain waiting to be sacrificed. We almost burst with the tension. Finally we opened the tabs and Edward, the house manager, went out. It was one of the most awful moments of my career. I did not really hear the announcement. I lost the will to live after, 'Ladies and Gentlemen, owing to the indisposition of . . .' All I heard was booing followed by polite British applause for the 'underdog', as they learned that the 'understudy' was to be given his chance. There was understandably widespread disappointment among those who would not see their hero that day.

As we were recovering from this and getting ready to start the show, the pass door swung open. I joked that it was the conductor escaping already but as I turned I saw that it was Mikhail Baryshnikov looking for Rudolf. He asked me if he could go to Rudolf's dressing-room and I walked him towards the swing doors.

Following in Rudolf's footsteps, Baryshnikov had defected from Russia in 1974. He was younger than Rudolf, very pretty, and they were ballet rivals. Baryshnikov was also Jewish. As Rudolf was Muslim, there was not a lot of love lost on Rudolf's side. His anti-Semitism was well known, although I had only experienced the full blast of his feelings about anyone privately. Rudolf certainly would not have wanted to dance in front of his rival when under par, or maybe he just didn't want to dance in front of him at all.

Just as we got to the doors, through the glass panels we saw the back of Rudolf exiting very quickly into the afternoon air. I am sure that this was no coincidence and that on hearing that Baryshnikov was in the audience, Rudi's ankle probably got worse.

Edward, the front-of-house manager, returned to the front of house to brace the box office for complaints and refunds. Somehow the energy was taken away from us. Though it was a successful show, there was definitely something vital missing.

It was stated proudly in the programme: 'Nureyev will dance at every performance.' There had never been any reason up until now to doubt it. That same year, Rudolf cancelled with Boston Ballet in America as well.

We had a change of mood for the second part of the Nancy season. There was a new programme, including *Songs Without Words*, *Songs of a Wayfarer*, *Symphony in D*, and for the first time in the UK, Nureyev in *Miss Julie*. Dark and powerful, it was a totally new experience to see Rudi acting and dancing in this wonderful piece. I would describe the experience as like watching someone with a silent role in a movie managing to totally steal the show from anyone else, it was so utterly transfixing every time he moved or appeared upon the stage.

I liked the way that a lot of the stagehands watched the shows fully aware that, however cynical they were about Rudi, they were part of a very special experience.

The 1983 season ended without any further cancellations or incidents.

I had a rather different year in 1984. On a gloomy Sunday in June, the Coliseum box office opened very early for an unusual distribution of tickets. A row of coaches lined St Martin's Lane, and groups of people were huddled around their suitcases clutching cups of coffee.

It was a very big day. The English National Opera was off on a ground-breaking tour to the USA. It was their first tour to the States and there was no Nureyev Festival, as Rudolf was appearing on Broadway in a season entitled *Nureyev and Friends*.

Walking away from St Martin's Lane, watching the loaded coaches disappear for their adventure, I was about to start the summer season working with fabulous companies: London Festival Ballet, Dutch National Ballet and Dance Theatre of Harlem.

At this time I was working in the technical office, not as a stage manager, and as such was not required on the tour to the USA. I found myself volunteered as the responsible adult in charge, named on the licence of the theatre and on a steep learning curve about how the other side of this theatre worked. I knew my backstage world very well, but to be in the public eye and with a new side to learn about, from loos to programmes, it was a little daunting.

In my briefing on the day-to-day running of the theatre, I had a speed-learning session on ice creams, programmes, safety checks and complaints. Luckily, little of this ever took up any of my time again.

Every night we rehearsed the evacuation procedure for clearing the audience. But I was lucky: we never needed to do this for real that year. If this had been a little earlier, I would have had the worry of the IRA bomb threats. My memories of evacuating that huge theatre during the mid-'70s and early '80s, sometimes four times a night, were common to most people who worked in London theatres during that period. In 1975, just after the bombing of the London Hilton on Park Lane, there had been a bomb warning about the Coliseum, using the same codeword that had been used for the Hilton. I don't think any of us had ever been so scared as the army turned up to search the theatre. Now, whilst we were still keeping a close eye out for abandoned briefcases and ticking suitcases left in the cloakrooms, there was not that constant sense of disquiet that we had all once endured.

I had spent years waving at people in Festival Ballet as I went about my work on operas; it was wonderful now to be working with them and meeting the dancers. I watched ballets new to me, like

Pulcinella and my first *Polotsvian Dances* (from *Prince Igor*). This was a slightly old-fashioned piece, with singers crammed into the side boxes beside the stage. Week after week of ballet season stretched in front of us. I was very happy, even if there was no Rudolf Nureyev to keep us all on our toes.

Then Dutch National Ballet was on stage for their first rehearsal. This was a big season for them and a major first night. I was showing their stage manager how to use the lever for the house curtain. I lowered the curtain and showed them how to 'bounce' the curtain for full stage calls. We did this every day. But this time there was a rumble, then a huge explosion of masonry and we all ran in fear for our lives. It was like an earthquake.

The piston for the hydraulics that operated the house curtain had jumped its cradle and gone through the masonry of the proscenium arch. The curtain was stuck with the hanging bar halfway to the floor, cutting the view of the stage horizontally in half.

It was not a pretty sight. It looked terminal, expensive and a big problem.

We stood there in stunned amazement. People began to ask me, 'What did you do?' Well, nothing, I just pulled the handle as usual. The atmosphere was a little tense and the problem was about to get very expensive. Dutch National Ballet did not get their vital stage rehearsal on their first day. They were crammed into a rehearsal room whilst engineers ran against the clock to get the stage and the curtain up and running for the evening. The vast turquoise house curtains were lifted from their jammed midway position just in time for the evening's performance. But for the next two nights of this lovely season, a rather dull set of 'blacks', black velour curtains, were flown in and out without much glory. Well, at least it hadn't happened on a Nureyev Festival night. I would not have liked to explain it to Rudi.

It was terrible to be the one who had simply pulled that lever once too often. Trying to find some consolation, we all said, 'Thank heavens it didn't happen during a show.' Even the visiting company seemed relieved about this, but it had been a stressful day for them.

Their first night was fascinating. This was modern ballet close up for me and it was riveting. There was an interesting piece performed by a female dancer to a solo on-stage piano, lit by a single follow spot hand held on stage. Her body was fascinating: she looked like a bodybuilder, with enlarged muscles and etched sinews. She was a totally different shape to a classical ballet dancer.

The third company arriving for our entertainment was the Dance Theatre of Harlem. They all seemed to be tall, elegant and fabulous looking, and they were all very friendly. They had a wonderful repertoire and there was a surprise in store for me as well.

I had assumed that none of the 'old crowd' would be around. But Robert Tracy was there too, working for Dance Theatre of Harlem as special events coordinator.

Rudolf was on Broadway with *Nureyev and Friends*, starring Rudolf and invited guests, and Robert had decided to give this a wide berth. He said that it was organised too late with no planning and it was destined to be a disaster. Which it was, 'both financially and critically'. Robert had decided to stay in St Tropez and finish his book on Martha Graham, then go on to London as special events organiser.

It looked as though there really would be no Nureyev in my life this year at the Coliseum, but we were to meet later in Paris.

The Dance Theatre of Harlem's programme was wonderful. *Giselle* performed with these beautiful dancers, some of the girls being over 6 ft tall, put a whole new perspective on my vision of the world of ballet. Their 'voodoo' ballet *Banda* mesmerised full houses and everyone backstage with its whistles, drums and sense of mysterious threat. It was a sell-out, with all of us crew members and office workers crowded into the doorways at the back of the stalls. I learned after the first rehearsal that, to get the full effect, this performance was one that had to be watched and absorbed from the front.

One particular moment stands out in my memory. There was an entrance from the wings of all the female dancers in their Haitian skirts, white blouses and brightly coloured turbans that I will never forget. Somehow they walked in on their knees, holding their skirts up in front of them. Their fluidity was incredible and they appeared to have an extra joint mid-calf, as they effortlessly crossed the stage. It was electrifying. With Harlem's spectacular *Firebird*, the 1984 season ended.

It was not until many years later that I read about the friendship or relationship between Rudolf and Arthur Mitchell of the Dance Theatre of Harlem.

The ballet season drew to a close and now a second Russian was to dominate my life. Yuri Lyubimov, a huge, larger-than-life figure, ruled a 'who's who in British theatre' company that had been pulled together for a production of Dostoyevsky's *The Possessed* at the Almeida Theatre.

Originally from the Taganka Theatre in Moscow, Yuri had been used to long rehearsal periods sometimes of up to four months. This was unheard of in England. We were used to three weeks in a rehearsal room before moving on to the stage. There was another difference as well. In Russian tradition, every single move had been pre-plotted, worked out so that there was no room for any instinctive or intuitive movement but plenty of room for confrontation. The British cast, asking instinctive questions about what they had been asked to do, were basically told to 'just get on with it'. It was a fascinating insight into the world that Nureyev had come from, with its rigid discipline and routine.

I had experienced this type of production just once before with Joachim Herz's production of Richard Strauss's *Salome*. This stretched everyone to their limits and intelligent actors like Josephine Barstow met the might of a goliath who would tell her where she was going to be at every beat of every bar. No questions, no flexibility.

It was like a movie mapped out on storyboards, yet this was for a live art form. We all had to get used to hours of rehearsals, where John the Baptist would just sit on the floor at the front of the stage whilst intricate movements and placements of slaves, courtesans and courtiers were moved across from one part of the set to another. There was never any question about not calling anyone for a rehearsal. They all had to be there.

Yuri Lyubimov came from the same school of directors. The piece was pre-plotted, mostly to music, and, again, there appeared to be no flexibility. The ten-week rehearsal period started in a freezing cold hall in Peckham, south-east London, then moved to that wonderful but small theatre, the Almeida in Islington.

The cast was very weighty: 17 of Britain's best-known actors were taken to their limits. As company manager, so was I, and everyone else who worked on the production. People resigned, threatened to resign, did not turn up or threatened not to. Agents were called and meetings were held. It was very stressful.

Two of the cast were inspired in desperation one night, to create 'the bottle chart'. All our names were written on this wonderful sheet. You could collect points for whatever you did – threatening to call your agent, losing your temper, hiding in the loo and pretending to call your agent. Bottles referred to 'bottling out' or chickening out of doing the show. It was a clever release mechanism for any pent-up frustrations. It lifted everyone out of their solitary confinement and made us a team. Even Yuri's name was on there, along with Anna's, his interpreter and assistant. One day, someone gave Yuri thousands of points, which caused the wonderful quote from Anna, 'Yuri loves you so much. Why you give him so many bottles?'

After a short season at the Almeida, which was more like a preview run, we left for an unusually glamorous tour – to Paris, Bologna, Reggio Emilia and Milan, before heading back to the Almeida for another run. It was a very successful production that ended on a high note, being filmed by Channel 4. We had a filled bottle chart, which had to be explained many times over, as we proudly put it up at the stage door everywhere we went. Lunacy and fun.

There were some amusing moments while travelling with an established company of actors. I enjoyed this work, but missed the dance world. On about our second or third performance of the three-week season of *The Possessed* in Paris, it only took seconds for the whisper to go round the auditorium, 'Noureïev!' One of our cast peeked out through our strange, black elastic-walled set, designed by Stefanos Lazaridis, spotted him and spread the word to all of us backstage.

I found Rudolf in the interval at theThéâtre National de l'Odéon and, like Robert all those years earlier after their first meeting, I thought he was joking when he said that I should come and see him.

A tortuous exchange of addresses and phone numbers followed between the two of us, surrounded by milling curious members of the audience. His entourage, who looked just like the ones in London, waited impatiently – beautiful young men looking on in mild annoyance at this female interloper on their patch.

I did not manage to see him again, however, as we had technical problems on the show, but Bill Akers provided me with a wonderful insight into the 'private' Nureyev in Paris and what I had missed.

'I was just passing through Paris getting some designs checked and, to be honest, I thought that I was going to get away with not seeing him. I was on an incredibly tight schedule and when I had phoned his office at the Paris Opéra, they said that he was in Italy. I left my name and thought that this was quite lucky in a way. Of course, just as I was leaving my hotel room the next morning, my phone rang and this voice said, "What are you doing? You are trying to avoid me."

'I said, "Of course not, but I thought you were in Italy."

'"No, in Paris. Come and join me, we will go somewhere unobtrusive for a coffee."

'Slightly reluctantly, as I had so much to do and really did not need this, I went to the Paris Opéra and there he was in that huge fur coat that hung from the shoulders down to the ground with a train, and that huge hat. He said, "Darling, we will go somewhere unobtrusive."

'Unobtrusive! We ended up at the Café de la Paix. As if there is anywhere less unobtrusive in the whole world!

'When we walked in, you could tell that the head waiter hated him and Rudi said to him, "We want to sit somewhere unobtrusive, like in the window."

'Whilst we were sitting there, people were knocking on the window and waving to him. When I said to him, "I thought you said unobtrusive," he replied, "But this is Paris, you have to be seen. This has been happening to me all my life. Sit back, darling, and enjoy it."' Bill laughs at this story.

In Paris in '84, Nureyev presented Martha Graham's *Phaedra's Dream* to a mixed welcome, and *Romeo and Juliet* was premiered. His work as a choreographer and director of Paris Opéra Ballet was being admired and challenged.

Rudolf had been at Palais Garnier with the ballet for nearly a year and when reading about it, it does not sound like it was an easy time for anyone involved. According to Robert, even the language drove Rudolf mad, and he said that all they did was 'talk, talk, talk'. The politics overwhelmed Rudolf, who as both artistic director/choreographer and dancer, just wanted to mount and create new ballets for them.

His much-reported upheaval of the promotion system for dancers vaulted Sylvie Guillem and others out of the corps and to the étoile (soloist and star) status. Rudolf ignored the many levels that they had traditionally had to work their way through while hoping to be spotted and promoted. The stress began to show between him and the management of the Palais Garnier as he was working around the world dancing with other companies, and running a ballet company on the phone a lot of the time.

'It was wonderful that Rudolf was at Paris Opéra Ballet. He gave such precious advice. The dancers could not believe it that he joined the juniors for class. He was so hands on, not a desk man. There is not anyone who has come through the company during his time or since Rudolf who does not owe everything to him,' Violette Verdy told me.

With hindsight, however, it seems that 1984 was when it all really started to unravel. Rudolf was on Broadway, running Paris Opéra Ballet on his mobile, but getting dire reviews. People were now writing what they had been thinking and saying privately for a while. Rudolf appeared later with the *Friends* in Edinburgh, not London, and over the next few years when the London seasons seemed far away, he would be found everywhere from Cardiff to Canterbury in the UK. These were great touring theatres where the audience would be appreciative, but they perhaps lacked the cachet of the internationally renowned venues.

Violette and Robert told me that his friends stopped coming to see him dance during this period. They did not want to see him make a fool of himself and wanted to retain a pure memory of him dancing when he was at his peak.

'I think we all hoped that he would somehow get better. People were talking behind his back, saying that he could not jump any more. It was the start of the rejection. We all tried to keep it going for Rudolf. If he had dinner parties at the Dakota, we would all help, I even washed table napkins at home for these parties. This was to help him, really, to think things were still the same and maintain the old standards. Robert was living in the Dakota apartment – even when Rudolf was away with others on St Barts, Robert was still there. You know there was not anything that we would not have done,' recalls Violette.

CHAPTER SIX

Sugar

The back-cloth was magnificent. It was enormous, pale-blue and white, fragile. Its gossamer tissue, dusty and expensive, was a fairy-tale fabric stretching from one side of the stage to the other and we were about to try and set fire to it.

A lone figure stood on the centre of the stage. Behind him the magnificent cloth stretched the full width of the Coliseum stage. He stood in silhouette – a black outline against pale-blue – workman-like in his darker blue overalls.

The atmosphere was serious, quiet; there was no music, only voices talking about the day's work and the checklist for the evening.

The sound of a television set coming from the fly floor jarred against the conversations on the stage. Wimbledon fortnight was with us again. Loud groans, shouts of ecstasy and 'Come on Navratilova' floated down as we stared at the back-cloth. It was for *Swan Lake* and it was a work of art.

Over on the prompt side, stage left of the vast, open, black lino-covered stage, a group of men were standing around what looked like a pair of rusty oil drums. A lot of heel rocking was going on. An official-looking peaked-capped man looked on in astonishment at this very low-tech version of a dry-ice machine. Take two oil drums, fill with water, then add two large metal paddles lowered in on rope. Allow to boil for while. Then drop in the dry ice. It defeated even the eagle eye of the fire inspector. However hard he tried, he could not actually find a reason why it should not be used. It was arcane, it worked, but it was terrifying to look at.

A sole ballerina joined us on stage. Various crew members were walking around her, but she was focused, in her own world. As she pirouetted, her T-shirt flashed the words 'Frankie says' and 'Relax' over and over again like a flashing neon sign. Even after a three-hour rehearsal she wasn't satisfied or ready to stop.

It was the start of the 1985 season. Matsuyama Ballet, Tokyo, was with us and so was Rudolf Nureyev.

I had had enough of 'Frankie' whirring round at me and left the stage. On my way out into the London air, I waved at Rudi as I went past his room. He beckoned me in. We hadn't spoken socially yet this season.

'What have you been doing?' Rudolf asked.

'I've been in Hammersmith and Billingham again.' He looked bemused at the mention of Billingham, so I explained, 'It is in the North-east, great people, not a great place.'

'Cold?' he queried.

'Sometimes.' I had an image of me standing in the rather forlorn square in the centre of the town, its requisite statue in pride of place, trying to decide whether to eat at the Chinese or the fish and chip shop. Those were the only choices. A huddled bald-headed figure walked past me in an overlarge sheepskin coat, bundled up against the cold. This was the film star Donald Pleasance wandering around the town, trying to find something, anything, to do in the spare hours before the show on performance days. Usually we all had to settle for battling against the searing wind and cold.

'Sounds like Siberia,' Rudolf joked.

'The people have a fantastic accent, sometimes difficult to understand.'

'No, sounds like Paris,' Rudolf said. And then he roared with laughter.

'I thought that you were having a good time? I have been reading some great reviews.' I hadn't actually read anything but I thought it would be appreciated if I said I had. During the endless rounds of dressing-rooms each night, you could be forgiven for creating conversation and showing interest when you had run out of the usual

'Done anything interesting since last night?' Talking to Nureyev was a different case, of course, but I still felt that I should perhaps have known more than I did about what he had been doing between the seasons.

'Well, you know how it is. But I am here now and we must get on.'

'May a friend of mine, Harriet, watch today? She would love to meet you. You saw her in Paris in *The Possessed*.'

'Which one was she?'

'Maria, the cripple.'

'She was very good.'

'Thank you, she will be thrilled.'

I knew Harriet was going to be pleased and immediately phoned her to tell her the good news.

'I danced with Rudolf Nureyev,' Harriet Walter recalled. We were sitting in the brand-new foyer of the Hampstead Theatre Club in Swiss Cottage. It was another one of those meetings between two people who have not seen each other for a long time. Nearly 18 years had passed since we first met on *The Possessed* at the Almeida.

Sometimes I forget what effect Rudolf had on so very many people. Not just the fans but also on other performers and would-be performers.

Harriet remembers wanting to go on the stage from the age of nine. Her mother and grandmother used to take her to the ballet, but it was at the age of eleven, after seeing Rudolf Nureyev for the first time, that Harriet made what she called an 'internal connection' of some sort. 'Nureyev's art as a performer, his passion and his musicality, became the focus of my inspiration,' said Harriet.

When Harriet talked about this moment, her fist went instinctively to her gut. It was a gut pull that made her act and had connected Nureyev to her.

Harriet remembered Rudolf coming to watch a production of *Hamlet* at the Old Vic in London, in which she appeared. Because there was no defined reason to meet him, she says that she hid in the lavatory until he had gone. She did not know what to say or do and how to maintain her dignity if she came face-to-face with Nureyev, so she had hidden from him.

But dancing with Nureyev?

'I know it sounds implausible,' recalls Harriet, 'but it was at a charity ball for kids and teenagers. I must have been about ten.'

'There was a rock group playing. I don't know who they were. During the evening we all noticed this young guy with shaggy hair dancing to the side of the stage. He was pirouetting, 'showing off' in our eyes, and just generally attracting attention to himself. It was that time in the '60s when the conga was the thing to do at parties, where you all followed one another round the room with your hands round each other's waists.

'In my memory, I am trotting along at the head of the line and this young guy with the shaggy hair pushes in behind me, grabs my waist and says, "Let's go." When I asked afterwards who he was, they said he was a young Russian dancer who had just come over to join the Royal Ballet. There weren't that many. It must have been Rudolf.'

On the day Harriet came to the Coliseum, I remember watching her walk hesitantly on to the stage. Rudolf was at the barre and I introduced Harriet to him. She seemed cautious. It must have been a heart-stopping moment to meet this embodiment of your inspiration, the reason you are on stage today, the person who had basically confirmed your career path and journey.

Harriet explained, 'At boarding school, whilst the other girls had posters of the Rolling Stones or The Beatles on the walls of the dormitory, my own bit of the wall was a shrine to Nureyev. But he was so much more than a pin-up, beautiful though he was. I had seen *Romeo and Juliet* three or four times and would disappear to the music room at night to play my record of it, alternating between "being" Fonteyn and Nureyev. Significantly, it wasn't accuracy of execution that I tried to achieve but a recreation of the acting performance. As an actress you watch people, and whenever I meet old school friends I know what their gestures are going to be, how they will look or what their arms will do. When I met Nureyev, I knew what he was going to look like and what his body looked like from all the years of watching him. It was an extraordinary and uncanny thing to be watching those same memorised movements from the wings of the Coliseum.

'I was surprised how delicate he looked, powdery almost. I remember looking at the freckles on his shoulder and looking at those extraordinarily pale doe-like eyes.

'We talked briefly about Lyubimov, the director of *The Possessed*, not something that one can be brief about. I was tongue-tied, as I was desperate not to appear a gushing mad fan. So I went to the other extreme of being super-cool and probably seemed indifferent or just plain boring.

'As I backed away, sensing that the conversation was at an end and aware that he was working, warming up and concentrating, he stopped me with, "You know Solzhenitsyn?"

'"Yes," I replied.

'"He is crazy too." And that was it, I thought, meeting over. I felt that this had been a lost opportunity, but what did I expect? Such is the nature of these meetings – which are momentous for one person and insignificant for the other. Someone once described meeting the Queen and said, "It wasn't amazing that I was meeting the Queen, it was amazing that she was meeting me." That came quite near to my experience.

'There seemed to be a gap between what was going on in his head and what was going on in front of him, as if he didn't want to get too close. I didn't have anything to offer him, so this friendship was not going to go much further than this.

'During the performance, I was surprised that he came up to me to speak to me when he had a break backstage. I was trying to be as invisible as possible, as I know how off-putting it can be to catch sight of onlookers in the wings. But he would stride over and make some comment about the performance. At one point, while practising a jump he said to me, laughing at himself, "This cow needs a trampoline."'

I am not surprised by the fact that he did this: after all, they were both performers and Harriet had presented herself to him as a performer, not a love-sick fan.

Harriet continued, 'In the dressing-room after the performance, I gabbled out my thanks and congratulations and he pooh-poohed me. I wanted to say, "Yes, I know. I'm not ignorant. I know you are past your best and I did see you at your best, but you are still a unique actor and I was moved to tears." But, of course, I didn't say any of that, instead I cringingly asked for an autograph. I still have it, in feeble biro and smudged with sweat.'

I told Harriet that I had not met anyone who hadn't succumbed at some point and asked for his autograph. It seems that we are all the same when it comes to meeting one of our idols.

Harriet left that evening with an invitation from Rudolf to come again. I was pleased, too, as it gave me someone to talk to as well during the evening and it was always nice to welcome friends and show them round.

At this time, Rudolf wanted a copy of the English stage version of *The Brothers Karamazov*, which he had heard of. Harriet told Rudolf that she knew some of the actors who had been involved in the production and promised to get hold of a copy for him.

She returned the following week to watch again and gave a copy of *Karamazov* to Rudolf. The tragedy was that it was a much-loved copy belonging to Stephen Boxer. He had kept it following an arduous trip to Georgia with Alan Rickman and many others. It was marked up with moves, thoughts, remarks and memories. Rudolf never returned it.

Harriet and I both knew what something like this means to a performer. It would have held so many memories and we wondered where it had ended up – in a box of memorabilia or just in a bin. It is very sad to think of this. I failed to get it back on so many occasions as Rudolf was 'still reading it' or it was in another country.

Harriet met Nureyev one other time.

'I was appearing at The Pit [one of the theatres at the Barbican in London] and *Les Miserables* was playing in the main house. This was before it transferred to the West End. I was leaving with a friend and I saw Nureyev across the other side of the huge foyer walking towards us. He had obviously just come from seeing *Les Miserables* and was rushing to avoid the crowds and limos that were gathering outside in the street. I plucked up my courage as I approached and said "Hello." There was an instant of surprise – suspicion or lack of recognition – before he smiled and remembered who I was. He asked me if I was performing in the building and seemed vaguely interested when I told him that I was playing a medieval lesbian witch in a play by Howard Barker.

'As we moved away and my companion was about to demand how I knew him, Nureyev interrupted from the top of the stairs to ask, "Have you seen *Les Miserables*?"

'"No," I answered. "What did you think of it?"

'"Sugar," he replied. And off he swept. He was a man of few words.'

Back in London in 1985, on my way backstage I was given a message. It asked if I would visit Yoko Morishita, the prima ballerina, in her dressing-room, so I stopped at number-two dressing-room to see what she wanted.

When I watched Yoko Morishita or Lucette Aldous or any of the tiny dancers that Rudolf adored dancing with, I saw a beautifully dressed dancer at the top of her profession. I had no real clue what they endured. Of course, I saw them at class and then at performances, but I had no idea the hammering a dancer could get by being caught by spinning legs or arms during a performance. Bill Akers described them each as a 'gift-wrapped mighty mouse'.

When I walked into Yoko's dressing-room, I saw her tiny muscular legs covered in black bruises. It was a shock. I had watched young male dancers learn the hard and very painful way to judge the distance of a ballerina's outstretched leg. I did not realise that the ballerina suffered as well.

They asked me if I would go and buy something for her bruises, so I went out on a mission to buy witch hazel for her. But she was dancing again that night and I realised it must have been an on-going problem. I'm not sure when they would ever have got a chance to heal.

Although I had now spoken to people who had all known Rudolf in various ways, I had not spoken to anyone who had danced with him. Yoko Morishita was one of the constants during the '80s at the Coliseum. With other guests and stars of the visiting companies, she had experienced quite a lot with Rudolf.

I wanted to know what it was like as a dancer to be on stage with Nureyev, and what it was like to learn with him and to learn from him.

We exchanged e-mails between Suffolk and Tokyo.

'Yoko, how did you meet Rudi?'

'I first met him in 1976. I was practising with Marika Besobrasova in Monte Carlo. Rudi adored Marika and treated her like his second mother after he had gone into exile. As you know, Rudi had a villa in Monaco and one day when he was on holiday there, he arrived at Marika's and we practised together.

'He was so charming and very sexy. I am not saying that he was just handsome, you could see his wonderful warmness and generosity just oozing from him. This is what he looked like to me.

'I was thrilled, as he had read my reviews from my debut in New York with American Ballet Theatre. After rehearsing that day in Monaco, he invited me to dinner at his villa. We discovered during the meal that we were both appearing in the same gala at the Kennedy Center in Washington in April 1976.

'Then, by chance, the ballerina who should have been dancing with Rudolf was sick, and the night before they asked Rudolf if he would dance with me. He said "of course" and that is how I got to dance with Rudi for the very first time. We performed the grand pas de deux from *Corsaire*.

'He taught me this role so gently and kindly that I did not feel nervous to be with him, learning from him. He taught me the variation in a lot of detail. Afterwards, he was very pleased with the performance. He said, though, that he could feel how nervous I had been from my hands.

'I had never dreamed of dancing with such a legend like Rudolf Nureyev. Of course, I felt nervous during the performance, but I appreciated his kindness in teaching me so many things. Now, beyond the nervousness, it seems like a dream.'

'When I met you and you were partnering Rudolf, during the '80s, he was, as Robert puts it, on the "downside of the ecstasy". How did you feel about dancing with him?' I asked Yoko.

'I believe that I have been dancing ballet as a mission gifted from God. The encounter with Rudolf was one of the wonderful events in my ballet life. The fact that he was past the peak of his ballet career had no impact on how seriously he took ballet and how hard he danced in order to tell people that ballet is the most wonderful thing to give you pleasure.

'Rudolf never begrudged teaching me everything he knew, and in many ways he gave me so many things from his heart. He gave me so many important things in ballet: how ballet can tell you how to live a life as a human and how to give pleasure to people through ballet.

'Rudolf was a wonderful man. He knew that I wanted to learn everything from him and I think that is why he treated me so well.'

'What was it like dancing with him, Yoko?'

'Whenever I was with him on stage, I felt so good. My worries disappeared when I danced with him. From dancing with him I gained a sense of inward security.

'I still dance now. It has been 52 years since I started ballet. I do not think that many people have danced this long in the world. I still do more than 70 shows a year. Full-length ballets. Without the support of so many people, I could not do this. Meeting such great people such as Dame Margot Fonteyn and Rudolf Nureyev has helped to make this possible. If I had not met them, I would not be able to dance now.'

Yoko and I first met in 1980 with Zurich Ballet, and Yoko remembered Dame Ninette de Valois coming backstage to see the company just before the photograph was taken.

'After the show, Dame Ninette asked me, "Tell me, who is your teacher?"

'Rudolf was standing just next to me and he said to Dame Ninette, "It's me." He looked so delighted and proud. It was so wonderful and I shall never forget that moment,' recalls Yoko Morishita.

In 1985, Matsuyama Ballet, Tokyo, was being put through its paces by our safety regulations.

London still poses a number of challenges for visiting ballet and theatre companies. For instance, we have very strict fire regulations that somehow always seem to come as a surprise to visitors. It does not matter how many times you ask about their fire-proofing, what the scenery is made of and what equipment they are bringing, it always seems to be a shock. Matsuyama Ballet, Tokyo, was no exception.

We seemed to have accepted their innovative dry-ice machines in an oil drum. Next on the test list were their delicate hangings and precious cloths. These had toured the world with them and were hung with care and precision. They were made of pure silk, measured about 30 metres square, and the crew and I knew that the fire officer from the local station would be visiting to test them.

When he did, he calmly took out a cigarette lighter and lit the corner of one of their precious cloths. There was disbelief on the faces of the ballet company's representatives. Even the most stoic was visibly shaken. This was truly 'trial by fire'.

Of course, this test was to check whether the cloth had sufficient fire-proofing. Legally, there was a time limit for how long the flame could last. More often than not in these cases, the flame continued well past the accepted limit. We all hoped that the cloths had been treated and that the flames would expire long before the limit was reached. It was always a difficult moment. The eyes of the visiting crew widened as it looked as if their valuably scenery was going to disappear in flames. It never did; it was snuffed out. But then we would have to explain that their cloths and scenery had failed the fire test and start the delicate negotiations to ensure that everything was made safe. It would all have to be sprayed before the show that night or the fire officer would condemn them and the show would not happen.

When the negotiations and explanations were over, we now had to fire-proof the priceless drapes and hangings.

This may sound like a straightforward task; in fact it was an urgent hurdle to get over. First came the problem of purchasing the flame retardant. Who had the money? Who was going to pay for it? Who would go out and get it? And finally who would pull the short straw to actually do the job? Whoever it was would spend hours drenching these cloths in the terrible-smelling chemicals, which, of course, dripped all over the stage.

Ted always seemed to end up doing this vile job. We would clean the lino floor, worry about whether it would dry in time for the show and then wonder if the delicate fabrics would hold the chemicals long enough to pass the inspection.

As Ted was usually still resplendent in his overalls and stinking of the chemicals when the fire officer returned, at least it proved that we had done it. The committee would form again in front of the fire officer as he solemnly attempted to 'disintegrate' the cloths. By this time, the audience was coming in and we were past the point of no return.

On this occasion, the first test was a success but, as if to tease us, he moved to a different hanging, one of the 'legs' – the smaller pieces that hung in front of the black masking flats to create the complete scene. We watched the cigarette lighter, then the flame. The suspense was awful.

'That is fine.' We all sighed, everyone shook hands and the first night of *Swan Lake* was safe.

Rudi came down into the wings, dropped his towel on the ground, stepped out of his clogs and nodded towards me.

'How is Old Galoshes tonight?' I asked.

He smiled, shrugged and replied, 'I am an average pair of galoshes tonight. Well, we'll see what this body can do.'

He looked tired certainly, his face slightly thinner, as was his hair, but the sparkle in the eyes was still there. Would the magic still be there?

Sometimes, that night, it was. Sometimes it was breathtaking and sometimes it was very rough. He rose to the challenge with Yoko as his partner again and he delicately supported this 'gift-wrapped mighty mouse'. When he could not pull out all the stops, he relied upon his soulful, fantastic acting skills. He re-enacted Violette's description of him: being neither male nor female and becoming a swan to dance with his swan.

In Act 1, he turned to the male corps de ballet and invited them to go hunting with him: with his hand on his hip saying to the lads, 'Why not join me?' This produced the required *sotto voce* laughter from all of us watching in the wings and sucked-in cheeks from Rudi. He got his response and he walked on to the stage with his team.

As I looked up from the prompt corner, a flock of Japanese swans disappeared up the wings, tutus bouncing, all the same height. It was an enchanting sight. And there, right in the middle of them, in a black suit and a dog collar, standing head and shoulders above the giggling swans, looking perplexed at the timing of his arrival, was the chaplain from St Paul's Church, Covent Garden, the 'actors' church'. He was on one of his regular visits to meet guest companies at the local theatres.

His arrival caused this flock of swans to hide their smiles with their hands as they giggled their way towards the double doors. God's representative on earth stood suddenly alone, blushing and bemused in the wings. I never had my camera with me at the right time!

I always watched the last scene of *Swan Lake* entranced. I would get swept up in the music and Rudi's intense searching. It made me hold my breath and the emotions used to well up and envelop me. Now, if I want to 'see' Rudolf again, I play the music for this final scene. The miracle works and somehow I really can see him.

It was the end of the first night, not a bad night. As I left the theatre, I followed some way behind Rudolf and a group of 'boys'. They left quickly – he hardly stopped at the stage door for autographs to the disappointment of the fans – and, once again, the brown TR4 roared off down Bedfordbury.

Rudolf's dressers and masseurs came and went. You could not blame them as they really did suffer from his tongue lashings. One night, when we were late as usual, I bent down to clear up some rosin by Rudi's clogs. It was in the way of the downstage entrance and I was concerned about it. Rudi shouted at me that this was 'not your job, he will do it', meaning his dresser.

I really did not care who cleared it away as long as someone did and we could start. Rudolf was furious with me for even touching it. All night he kept muttering to me that it was not my job. It was a long night.

This particular dresser was very French and called Alain. For the first time it seemed to me that Rudi had turned up with a man, not a boy or a 'plaything'. I do not know why, but he looked even less like a dresser than I do. He was tall, good looking and blond. He was always dressed immaculately, though casually, but certainly not for work backstage at a theatre. He looked out of place clutching a towel and Rudi's ever-present flask of tea.

Alain was also a consummate flirt. It was far too easy to become engrossed in talking to him and so not notice a famous pair of Tartar eyes watching every single moment, assessing what was happening.

The evening was running well, and Alain asked me if I knew of any good clubs to go to afterwards. I was not sure. It was not my scene but we were all used to showing a visiting company around, so I said, 'Yes, sure.' Then I was treated to a neck massage in the wings by this 'dresser' – deliberately, I should think, for his employer to see. A friend of mine, one of the crew and an ex-dancer with Australian Ballet, noticed this and said 'be careful'. It was a bit too late for that. Rudi had seen all of it.

At the end of the night, I chickened out of the club arrangement: it was late, I was not dressed for clubbing and maybe my sixth sense was trying to tell me that this was really not a very good idea. I sensed that a lot of assumptions were being made.

Of all the things that could have upset a working relationship, this was not one that I expected.

The next day Alain came to find me in the prompt corner. He told me that he had been 'locked' out last night. He was laughing as he explained that Rudi had set the alarms and so he could not get in. I think we both realised what Rudi had done and that he had done it deliberately.

I asked Alain where he had stayed, and he said he had gone to a hotel round the corner. My brain slowly worked out what was going on and what Rudolf must have thought had happened.

Oh, God, how could I explain this one? That I did not fancy him, really, and even if we had gone out nothing would have happened? I was so concerned. Professionally this was a hanging offence. I felt sick and had resigned myself to the fact that I could be waving goodbye to the Nureyev Festival in ignominy.

Rudolf arrived in the wings to find Alain and me finishing our conversation. I was devastated. He just stared at me, no words, nothing, just an ice-cold look. I was sent to Coventry, and for something that had not even happened.

I had no idea how we were going to get through the rest of the season. My face must have said it all. One of my colleagues from the promoters arrived on the stage and asked whether everything was all right. He got the whole story, poor man. I felt impotent and as though

I had been caught in flagrante when absolutely nothing had happened.

We spent the next few days in a mood of polite stand-off. Nothing had been said but somehow that felt worse. It was all civil, polite even, but non-communicative.

What a stupid thing to have happened; yet it was so innocent. Like all of us who knew him, I would never have done anything to hurt him. It was so sad.

Alain and I kept a low profile for a few days. I did not ask him what life at home was like with Rudi. I did not want to be seen talking to this man ever again. We kept our contact to furtive smiles and raised eyebrows in the wings.

I still watched every single moment of *Swan Lake*. I loved *Giselle*, *Petrouchka*, *Firebird* and all the ballets that I had experienced at such close quarters during these six years. But 'Duck Pond' always did it for me. Even the dance of the cygnets moved me, despite the number of times it had been parodied. In fact, this dance is incredibly difficult to get right. When I watched the dancers come off, it was interesting to note their reactions to their own performance: they were either giggling or cross about what they personally had got wrong during this pas de quatre. They looked beautiful on stage but when they came off stage into the wings they were dripping with sweat and breathless. Sometimes they were almost winded and people would rush to help them by holding their arms above their heads in order that they could breathe more easily.

I used to stand way back, halfway upstage right, or OP – opposite prompt – so that I could see the prompt corner in case anyone needed me, but could not easily be seen from on stage. There, I had a good view of the pass door and the dressing-room door, too. I could watch for intruders. One of Rudi's constant questions to me was, 'Who is that person?'

'Who? Where? Where are you looking?' I would ask.

He used to shrug his head over his shoulder to indicate where this poor soul was standing.

'They said they were a friend of yours.'

'No. I do not know them.'

This was very hard. More often than not I think he did know them but had changed his mind and found them irritating. I used to spend some time talking to them to see if I could find out more. When it seemed they had been invited, I sneaked them through to the front and slipped them in at the back of a box, so they could 'get a better view'.

Of course, there were some people who tried it on, but not many. Ralph and his colleagues at the stage door were difficult to get past, even if you worked there and they had known you for 20 years.

We have so many rules in the theatre. Like Bill Akers, I had been taught by one of the best, Robert Stanton at LAMDA. We learned that there was an unseen boundary where, for instance, Rudi could be Rudi in the wings, but as soon as he put a foot on the stage he became Mr Nureyev. This was something that outsiders always found strange but it becomes second nature eventually.

Watching from the wings is an art. There is a huge difference between gawping and watching, one that is difficult to explain to a non-theatre person. One night I was spotted. It was Act 3; I adored watching the final scene. I adored just standing and watching.

'You watch this every night?' Rudolf asked, sniffing, trying not to look too interested.

'Yes, I am sorry. Am I putting you off?' I was surprised that he was talking to me.

'No. I need it. It helps me.' We had made contact again, at last, after the Alain incident. It was an incredible relief.

In the last week of the season we changed ballets from *Swan Lake* to *Giselle*. Out went that beautiful cloth and in came the forest of *Giselle*. We had a quick change round with lighting and a short rehearsal for this wonderful piece.

I made no apologies for standing and staring during this ballet. I was not alone. I was one of a crowd watching Rudi as he laid that plastic bunch of lilies on a polystyrene grave. He did it over and over again during that week and each time we believed. We were all flushed with incredulity, asking ourselves that old question, 'How does he do that?' All he did was walk from upstage left down on a diagonal, a spectacular black velvet cloak falling in a train from his shoulders, to where the grave was, yet we were with him all the way. It was pure charisma. No circus, no leaps, or 'on-the-edge' dancing. Just sheer artistry, acting and being the part.

Pamela Foulkes remembers, 'He was gorgeous and he knew it. His arrogance was founded on the knowledge that he was beautiful and was an incredible dancer. But you know, I had so much respect for him because he cared about the whole show, not just his dancing. He watched every little thing. He watched the scenery, the lighting, everything, which I had to respect. Dancers do not usually do that, they are focused on their "bit" and they don't see anything else. He was focused on the whole effect. You had to admire him for that as well as his dancing and artistry.'

I was coming to the end of my Nureyev experiences and I asked Bill when he had last seen him.

'I did not see him for some time and when we next saw him it was the late '80s,' Bill recalled.

'Roger and I were both shocked at what he looked like. I was actually a bit miffed. He was on tour in Australia with *Nureyev and Friends* and this was the first time ever that I had not been asked to be involved. We were sort of prepared for his dancing as we had read some of the reviews. But I was not prepared for what he looked like. Whilst the press was not being that kind to him, there appeared to be some sort of *noblesse oblige* that they would not actually crucify him.

'I had a panic phone call asking me if I would go and help them with the lighting, it was 7 p.m. one evening. That same evening, anyway, we had arranged a meal for Rudi at the Ballet to entertain him. He was going to give his approval on the costumes and scenery for a revival of *Don Quixote*.

'I arrived to help and he was swearing at me saying that I had not been there – but I was not involved. One of the pieces was *L'Après-midi d'un Faune*. I had never actually lit this, although I knew it terribly well. Our workshops rustled up a rock for him, the plinth that he was to lie on, as he did not have one. During the interval he had to be helped up onto it. I watched this and I thought that although no one had actually said what the matter was, I had known someone with Aids and I was certain that this was what Rudi's problem was.

'Of course, after the show he was cursing me saying, "Pig, where were my projections?" The scenery was basically conveyed by lighting projections. And I explained that if he had asked me, I would have done it. We saw him safely to the Ballet – a 1 a.m. supper as we were so late. He was charming. He loved the sets and the costumes, so all was well.

'I had heard that he had been taking coaching from Jack Lanchbery in conducting. He was so musical this seemed like a wonderful thing for him to do. He seemed to have a talent for it.

'Then the next time I saw him was in late 1992. I took Ann Fraser, the designer, with me from London, to see Rudi in Paris. We needed his approval on some designs of hers. This was *Don Quixote* again.

'We turned up at that extraordinary apartment of his. It looked like a Russian baronial hall or something out of *Boris Godunov*. Everything was sculptured: the curtains, the chairs and that long low table that was just covered in the most magnificent bronzes. And, of course, that famous wall covered in male nudes, probably all incredibly valuable oil paintings.

'Ann was terrified at meeting him and I had said to calm her down, "Don't worry, he won't bite you, he'll be charming", crossing my fingers as I said this, of course.

'"Get her a drink, she looks terrified," Rudi told me.

'"I need a drink. I'm terrified too," I laughed.

'To break the ice a little, I said to Rudi that there was a small gap on the wall where all the oil paintings were, adding, probably unnecessarily, "There's room for a small one!"

'He said, "Who needs a small one, darling?"

'It did lighten the atmosphere and I headed for the kitchen, which had a strange sliding door that you operated by a button. All I could find was Babycham, of all things, so I came back in and gave that to Ann. I suggested to Rudi that we leave Ann to set up the model and he and I went into his bedroom.

'There was the largest television set or screen I have ever seen in there. We sat watching a video from Paris showing Rudi's choreography.

'I asked him why it was so dark to look at as you could not see the dancers.

'"You will change that Bill. You always bring me light."

'I asked him about his conducting and he said, "Some is good. Some is all right."

'"You cannot expect to be a star from day one, Rudi."

'"I was."

'We went back to join Ann. Rudi adored the designs and said, "I will conduct the first two performances", which was lovely, of course.

'He had the press coming to see him in the apartment, so he was concerned to get ready for them. Ann packed away the set and designs, and Rudi said that he was going to take a bath.

'He had this ludicrous bathroom, which was much bigger than the bedroom. The bath was a huge malachite thing about three feet deep and you had to climb steps to get into it. He looked so frail that I asked him if he would like some help. At first he said no, and then as he went into the bathroom he called for me to come in and help him, which I did.

'As I helped him up the steps and down into the bath, I saw just how thin he had become. This powerful, beautiful athlete. Someone I had known for 30 years. It was dreadful. I helped him sponge himself down and get out of the bath and towelled him dry. He put on this heavy Russian dressing gown with a floppy hat and I placed him on the settee ready for the press. I went to the door and invited them in.

'"Maestro is ready for you now." And I left.

'The next day I went back to see him. It was really only to tie up any loose ends and he said everything was fine and that he would conduct the first two performances.

'I could not believe the change in him overnight, from frail to really very ill. He looked like a totally different person. As I walked back to my hotel, I realised that not only was he never going to conduct those performances for us but also that I was probably never going to see him again.

'I phoned the Ballet in Australia as soon as I got to my hotel room and explained that, whilst we would all hope and pray for him, I doubted he would conduct for us.

'I cried that whole plane journey home.

'This is all very sad, I know. But you know, despite all of his impossibilities, we loved him because he was wonderful. If you work in the theatre or have a love of the theatre, you are always watching for that special person and when you find them, like Rudi, it drives everyone and you will do everything you can to help them, because of their commitment to the whole thing. He was so very special.'

Bill continued, 'He had incredible insight for someone so young. I think that sometimes he didn't understand where it came from either. He should have been so upset when we had rehearsed *Don Quixote* and *Raymonda*, and then we cancelled *Don Quixote* for Nice and the tour. We really couldn't afford to stage *Don Quixote,* even though we had rehearsed it. This would have been his first opportunity to stamp his mark on a ballet and, sure, he was upset, but he understood. We just didn't have the budget.

'Of course we did do his *Don Quixote* eventually and as you know it was filmed. It was a great success. But this awareness beyond his years came out again when we were looking to do a new *Sleeping Beauty*. We were shown the new designs. They were so far ahead of their time and we just weren't sure. I suggested to Peggy van Praagh that she ask Rudi what he thought. He looked at the designs and said that we should do a "proper" one before doing this. He adored modern design but he felt we should do a traditional classical version first. Well, we went with the modern one and it was well received, but Rudi was right. We went on to do a new but traditional version and it was such a great success. I think he surprised himself sometimes.

'I have seen better dancers since Rudi but none that came anywhere near the whole person that was Rudi. Thank heavens for film and television. One of our friends phoned us the other day to tell us that *Sleeping Beauty* was on with Rudi and Margot, and so due to the wonders of television these amazing people were back with us, both of them looking 16 and wonderful.'

Pamela Foulkes concluded by saying, 'The Australian Ballet dancers owe so much to him. He was very generous in his help to the dancers, either in class or during the show. He always had time to show a dancer what to do. He must have brought the male dancers forward by years with his artistry, and in the homogenous atmosphere of class where all are equal, he just was one of the company.'

I asked Yoko Morishita if there was one thing that she wanted everyone to know about Rudolf.

'I think that he was a person who was extremely strict with himself to dance his whole life, a real artist. He did not dance to show off his skill or to become famous. Never. That is why so many people went to see him on stage, and if he was on stage for a whole fortnight then they went to see him every single night. Because he danced truly for his very existence, for his whole being. I do not think I have seen a person like him who danced to that extreme. At the same time he was so soft, warm hearted and kind. Because he was so sincere, you could see such charm and a wonderful aura coming from him on stage.

'I am so lucky that I lived in the same generation as Rudolf and stayed with him till his very end. He always nurtured my talent. He used to call me "Yoko-Yoko".

'Whenever we were together, dining or working, he talked about ballet and nothing else. He respected wonderful prima donnas, ballerinas in the twentieth century. Women like Galina Ulanova, Dame Margot Fonteyn and Yvette Chauviré.

'I don't think I will meet such a man again in my life.'

Throughout the '80s, Robert Tracy had stayed with Rudi. Even when Rudi was in the Caribbean with other guys, Robert stayed at the Dakota Building apartment waiting to start the catalogue of Rudi's collection.

Rudi relied on Robert even then and there is a story from Robert about how Rudi phoned him from St Barts because the car they were using had a puncture and Robert 'had to fix it'.

'He had so many people with him who could have phoned a garage, but he asked me to fix it.'

I wondered if Robert felt that Rudolf had had any regrets?

'Definitely. He was embarrassed about Kenneth Greve. He was a Danish guy who looked like Erik Bruhn. Rudolf invited him to dance at Paris Opéra. Rudolf wanted him to play the Prince in *Swan Lake*. He was dancing with American Ballet Theatre at the time. He wasn't that good a dancer but Rudolf adored him because he looked like Erik and he was Danish, too. It was embarrassing to watch.'

At 6 ft 5 in. tall, blond and handsome, Kenneth became the sole object of Rudolf's attentions.

Robert continued, 'He was straight but Rudolf was besotted with him. Rudolf tried to put him into ballets and he just wasn't good enough. The ballet company even went on strike because Rudolf tried to cast him. He was trying to relive and re-create what he had with Erik. Everyone knew it, even Rudolf knew it. I wasn't there, thank God, but he started to coach him and it wasn't working. Kenneth wouldn't have sex with Rudolf and Rudolf, in his fury and frustration, just started destroying the farm in Virginia where they were both staying.'

If you have dedicated 14 years of your life to one person, there must be moments when you look back and wonder what you would have or could have changed. I asked Robert if he had any regrets.

'You're kidding. I'm still here, aren't I? My work goes on, I'm writing my books and as a dance historian I couldn't have had a better teacher than Rudolf.'

I thought the end of the life of his lover and partner must have been awful for Robert. He had by that stage discovered that Rudi had left him £500 a month in his will and had decided to sue his friend for palimony.

Violette Verdy and I talked about this terrible time and she had an interesting viewpoint that maybe there is a type of 'madness' that occurs, rather like a syphilitic madness that makes you lose your sense of judgement and reasoning, and she thought that is what had happened to Rudi when he was making his will.

But Robert stayed with him even through the court case.

'I said that I would stay with him throughout the odyssey, which I did, except for that last month, when I couldn't get to see him.'

'You mean they, the Nureyev Foundation and friends, wouldn't let you see him?'

'Sure, but I understood.'

I am not sure that I would have taken this so well.

Prevented from seeing his friend in Paris, Robert was offered tickets for *La Bayadère* instead. Robert passed them on to a journalist and went to a punk concert. He is matter-of-fact about all this, as if there was nothing he could have done about it and, anyway, it is in the past. He understands.

Rudolf died on 6 January 1993. I wanted to know what Robert

had done, how he had coped with all his sadness. Did he go to the funeral? He almost laughs in astonishment. 'No way! I don't do funerals, and anyway it was a circus and Rudolf hated circuses. I didn't think he wanted to be buried either, so I was not going to go anywhere near that.'

Obviously 'circus' was their term, as it was used over and over by them and invoked by Robert to describe even Rudolf's funeral and again when he heard my description of the Royal Ballet's tribute to Rudolf in April 2003. Based in New York at the time, Robert had been unable to attend.

There were wonderful world-class dancers performing in front of video images of Rudolf. You could feel all of us torn between the live action on stage and the riveting, exquisite footage of Margot and Rudolf. Then there were pictures of Rudolf and Erik, but behind the most compelling dancers. It was too difficult for me and frustrating.

'Rudolf always said that you couldn't look at two things at once,' said Robert.

This performance had a huge impact on me, from the moment the house lights went out and Erik Mukhamedov read from (*Eugene*) *Onegin* over a huge flown picture of the young Nureyev. I missed the whole of the first item, which was Mukhamedov dancing, as I had tears streaming down my face. It was very powerful.

I described to Robert who had been there, who I had seen on the first night and then what happened when I was leaving.

At the bottom of the escalators there were two stunningly dressed Italian women. They stopped in front of a large photo of Rudolf. They paused and then bowed in front of it. It was a private and special moment. Not for show, but for themselves and for Rudolf. Robert thought that this was a beautiful moment. It was. Ten years after his death and Rudolf Nureyev stills commands such huge, deep feelings of loss.

What happens after spending 14 years of your life with someone?

'What did you do with yourself, Robert, after that time and how did you grieve?'

'I hibernated. I had to stay away from the funeral and all that. They had no idea what my relationship was like with him. They saw it here and there, not continuously. I wanted to say to them "What about at 3 a.m., 4 a.m., when he was being impossible, playing Bach all night, when he couldn't sleep?" They had really no idea. I travelled around Europe and started to write again. I wrote seven books in as many years. It took a long time to move on again.'

'What was Rudolf's legacy?'

'His choreography and, as I said before, his emancipation of the male dancer. He created so many more opportunities for dancers.'

Rudolf created more and more solos for men and balanced the major ballets. I would have thought that dancers today would have owed Rudi a lot but when I said this to Robert he was scathing. 'When they are interviewed, even the ones that worked with him at the Paris Opéra, they never mention Rudolf. They always mention Baryshnikov. It's as if Rudolf never existed. Some of the younger ones owe everything to Rudolf.'

'Is there anyone coming along who will replace Nureyev?'

'Malakhov, definitely. He is at the Berlin Opera and has just completed a full-length ballet version of *Ballo in Maschera*.'

'What would Rudolf have done next?'

'He wanted to visit China to teach there.'

After ten years, I wondered how often Robert still thought about Rudolf?

'He is in everything I do. I have two of the Richard Avedon photos of him by my bed. I mention him in everything I write. I dedicate my books to him and refer to his artistry and his legacy in every book.

'He is everywhere.'

Last week I ended up back in my garage sorting through programmes, this time in the heat of an unusual Suffolk summer. It was far too hot to be rummaging around thousands of programmes in a box that I had labelled 'My Brilliant Career!' Over 30 years of amazing people, operas, music, plays, orchestras, movie stars, conductors, supermodels, designers, opera singers and Nureyev.

My life moved on. I watched where and when the Nureyev events were happening during the late '80s, but I never worked on any of them. I read the dreadful reviews and felt such sadness that 'it' could come to this and wondered why he didn't just stop, even though I could hear him say, 'What would I do if I did not dance?' I was amazed that he put himself through the rigours of touring *The King and I* and the risk of scorn over his singing.

In six months, so many memories had been evoked. I had found and talked to so many people who had shared with me their stories and feelings about this man.

The overriding impression of his impact is 'once met, never forgotten'. I heard tales of people, from hairdressers in Eastbourne who had met him walking to the theatre, when he 'flashed' at them, which seemed unlikely, to waiters.

Rudolf was very much loved and is still mourned ten years after his death – enough so to make people cry when they speak of him.

I had the great privilege of working with this icon. Nureyev or 'Noureïev', 'Old Galoshes', 'Randolf Near Enough', 'Rudolf Never Off' – I had seen him in all those guises. I loved talking to him, getting to know him, listening to his stories and being able to watch him night after night. I was so very lucky to have had the chance to do this.

I saw a proud consummate performer go on 'no matter what', to entertain us all even if he couldn't fly any more. He could act and still pull in the crowds, either with *Nureyev and Friends* or *The King and I*. People still watch his choreography, though Robert shared his frustration about companies reverting to the 'old' choreography rather than Rudolf's.

Through the friends and people he had met and 'touched', I learned about his physical defects, his hunting, drinking, eating, working, reading and his fear that he wasn't going to live long. I also had the fascinating experience of trying to sort out people's memories, listening to what they remembered and talking to them about what had been written before.

I watched this 'impossible' man who everyone instinctively describes in a base, animalistic way. I prefer Violette Verdy's description of Rudi: having to become the role as a 'method' dancer, to dance like a swan, he became a swan. But that was not all he could do. Rudi watched the lighting, the props, the workers, the dancers, the orchestra, the audience and everyone involved. He understood how it all fitted together, how important each aspect was to the final outcome, to him and his performance.

That is how he gained all our respect and our love and how we all endured the bad times.

Violette Verdy remembers, 'We were late going up, as usual! Rudolf was warming up at the barre.

'He saw I was watching him, and as he prepared to take his arm over his head and bend his back backwards in a beautiful arch, he looked at me and said, "Darling, the only things that I can arch nowadays are my eyebrows."'

Coda

10 AUGUST 1985

It was the last night of the season with Matsuyama Ballet and we were all showered with presents. I was clutching an armful of miniature Japanese soaps, toothpaste and shampoo when I stopped in the corridor up by the stage door to chat with my colleague. We exchanged the usual: thoughts on what the future held for both of us, our holidays, our work and life in general. There was always an air of uncertainty about the end of a run or the end of a tour. I could feel all of us putting a brave face on so that we did not worry about lack of work, or alternatively did not boast about work, especially if we knew that other people did not have any to go to. It was unsettling as people left with their cards, flowers and mementos of their stay. I was still on a high, though, not only from the performance that night but also from the end of another great season.

There was a bustle of people behind me and I could see expectant looks ahead of me from fans and guests waiting for Rudi.

I turned round to face him, to say goodnight and he stopped, took my face in his hands and kissed me 'full on', not on either cheek. It was really unusual and a shock. I must have looked surprised, too.

'Goodnight, Caroline, thank you,' he said to me.

'Bye. You take care.'

Rudolf walked towards the stage door.

My colleague said in a loud stage whisper, 'Aids', and, horrified, I turned round to berate him.

When I turned back, Rudolf had gone.

I never saw him again.

Bibliography

Only major sources have been listed

Aronson, Theo, *Princess Margaret,* Michael O'Mara Books, London, 1997

Bland, Alexander (ed.), *Nureyev: An autobiography with pictures, by Rudolf Nureyev,* Hodder and Stoughton, London, 1962

Bradford, Sarah, *America's Queen: The Life of Jacqueline Kennedy,* Penguin, London, 2000

Gladstone, Victor, *The London Coliseum*, Chadwyck-Healey/Somerset House, 1980

Haslam, Dave, *Manchester, England*, Fourth Estate, London, 2000

Mander, Raymond and Mitchenson, Joe, *The Lost Theatres of London*, Rupert Hart-Davis, London, New York, 1968

Solway, Diane, *Nureyev: His Life,* Weidenfeld and Nicholson, London, 1998

Watson, Peter, *Nureyev: A Biography*, Hodder and Stoughton, London, 1994

Index